Robot Makers

An Essential Guide to Choosing a Career in Robotics

CELESTE BAINE

Engineering Education Service Center

Eugene, OR

Robot Makers

An Essential Guide to Choosing a Career in Robotics

by Celeste Baine

Published by:
Engineering Education Service Center (an imprint of Bonamy Publishing)
1004 5th St
Springfield, OR 97477 U.S.A.
(541) 988-1005
www.engineeringedu.com

Publishers Cataloging-in-Publication Data

Baine, Celeste

Robot Makers: an essential guide to choosing a career in robotics/ by Celeste Baine.

Includes bibliographical references and index.

ISBN 13: 978-0-9819300-4-6 (pbk.)

1. Engineering–Vocational guidance–United States   2. Robotics–Vocational guidance–United States   3. Engineering Technology—Vocational guidance–United States   I. Title. II. Baine, Celeste.

How to Order:

Single copies may be ordered from the Engineering Education Service Center, 1004 5th Street, Springfield, OR 97477; telephone (541) 988-1005; Web site: www.engineeringedu.com. Quantity discounts are also available.

For Lane and Joe. Your inextinguishable commitment to students is a thing to behold.

Contents

Appendix

Other Engineering Career Publications by

Celeste Baine

Is There an Engineer Inside You?: A Comprehensive Guide to Career Decisions in Engineering

The Green Engineer: Engineering Careers to Save the Earth

The Maritime Engineer: Careers in Naval Architecture and Marine, Ocean and Naval Engineering (ebook)

Engineers Make a Difference: Motivating Students to Pursue an Engineering Education (ebook)

The Musical Engineer: A Music Enthusiast's Guide to Engineering and Technology Careers (ebook)

The Fantastical Engineer: A Thrillseeker's Guide to Careers in Theme Park Engineering

High Tech Hot Shots: Careers in Sports Engineering

Ideas in Action: A Girl's Guide to Careers in Engineering

www.engineeringedu.com

Preface

Author Celeste Baine calls herself an "Engineering Career Evangelist," and I would wholeheartedly agree. Over the last 17 years she has authored over 20 books and booklets on the topic of engineering careers and education, winning numerous awards for her work. In 2007, new to STEM outreach, I met Celeste at a technical conference. After just a few minutes we discovered a mutual passion for furthering STEM education, and the groundwork was laid for our future collaboration.

While serving as the marketing and outreach director for the Society of Naval Architects and Marine Engineers (SNAME), I took on the task of turning SeaPerch, an underwater remotely operated vehicle (ROV), into a national STEM educational program. Hoping to capitalize on Celeste's successful series on engineering careers, SNAME commissioned Celeste to write a book on marine engineering. "Maritime Engineering" remains an important resource for SeaPerch, students, educators and others interested in learning about marine-related engineering careers.

As SeaPerch grew, we continued our partnership with Celeste, and invited her to be the keynote speaker at our first SeaPerch Stakeholders Meeting. Over the years, we have partnered on important projects designed to educate students, teachers and parents on the possibilities of a career in engineering.

In 2011, SeaPerch found a new home with the Association for Unmanned Vehicle Systems International Foundation (AUVSIF). This move enabled SeaPerch to be part of a longer pipeline of student robotics competitions, and allowed SeaPerch students the opportunity to compete in RoboBoat and RoboSub along with students from around the world.

Celeste's latest effort, "Robot Makers," is a guide to careers in robotics. "Robots are our future and can change the world," says Celeste. Within these pages is a wealth of information about what careers involved in robotics would look like, what type of education is needed, and even what the salary ranges are. This book will be a valuable resource for any student considering a career in the field, as well as educators, guidance counselors and parents hoping to learn more about robotics.

When you read this book, I know you will learn. What I also know is that you will feel Celeste's passion for engineering education. What I hope is that some of this passion will be passed on to you, and that it will help us find the next generation of robotics professionals.

Susan Giver Nelson
Executive Director, SeaPerch
AUVSI Foundation

Author Acknowledgments: This book wouldn't be possible without the vision of Susan Giver Nelson. Her direction of the SeaPerch program and commitment to inspiring a robotic future is unparalled. Without Susan, the world of underwater robots would look much different. I'd also like to thank my peer reviewers, Lisa Freed, Bruce MacKender and Mary Lou Ewald. Without their encouragement and gentle persuasions, this book would not be all that it is today. Along the way, I also had some fantastic contributors: Joe Bogusky, Amanda Nixon, and Dr. Chris Jones. Your quotes and insights into the heart of robots and robotic applications were invaluable. I'd like to thank Joe Bogusky from Auris Surgical Robotics for his interview and company tour. You have come along way from Louisiana Tech. Thanks also go to Cindy North for her photo with the BAXTER robot. I'm eternally grateful to the many people I met and talked to along the way that encouraged me to keep digging, keep writing and reminded me about the importance of this book.

Edited by: J. K. Brooks Publishing, LLC, jkbrookspublishing.com

Cover design by: Amy Siddon

Introduction

Improving medicine, being on the cutting edge of technology, creating a healthier planet, and making life easier are all compelling reasons for becoming a roboticist. But even more than that, getting into robotics assures a lifetime of opportunities that are rich and plentiful. Robots are here and are changing the world. Applications to use robots are enormous. The careers that support the industry offer opportunities to be creative and are challenging, prestigious, and satisfying.

Robots are already doing much behind the scenes work, such as building cars and kitchen appliances, milking cows, and packaging food. Robots are used to help with housework by vacuuming and mopping floors. Wirelessly controlled helicopters and lifelike dolls, dogs, and cats are sold as toys. You may not see them every day, but within the manufacturing industry alone there are over a million industrial robots assembling, painting, moving, transporting, packaging, and building products that you use every day. Within the robotic field, job satisfaction is high. Those in the field are often overheard saying how much joy they receive when they design or build a robotic arm or leg that helps someone pick up an object or walk.

To better understand engineering and robotics, you need to think about it as a journey (a career) instead of a job. In this journey, you will always be working to make your inventions or designs better. This means that your designs will often be modified over time to meet the needs of society or to incorporate new technology. This continual refinement is what makes products and processes better.

Your cell phone is a good example of this "technology-in-motion" concept. It was only five years ago when cell phones were large and only made phone calls. Today, because engineers continued to make the phones and networks better, you can send and receive text messages, take photos, get email, surf the net, and download apps to do almost anything or instantly get almost any information that you need. Without engineers working on every part of this infrastructure, this would not be possible. The same is true with the design and development of robots.

The careers and opportunities in this field are endless as robots become more integrated into our culture. Many of the jobs you may see in the next ten years haven't even been invented. Many up and coming engineers will not only create new robots but new robotic sectors as well. Get your degree, get some experience, and be ready. The possibilities are endless for a motivated student.

Part I–What is a Robot?

You may know about robots because you watched a deadly cyborg try to take over the world on TV. Or, you are involved in or have seen a robotics competition, played with a Mindstorms LEGO set, or attended a science, engineering or maker event. Although you may not even recognize it as a robot, they have been around you for a long time. Advances in technology have refined what a robot does. New applications are continually expanding a robot's capabilities.

Although there are many definitions of a robot, in this book a robot is an electromechanical (i.e., mechanical parts that need electricity to operate) device that can react to its environment and perform operations either on a tether by remote control, autonomously by wireless or Bluetooth connections, or a hybrid of the two systems. The word robotics refers to learning and working with the design, construction, operation, and application of robots, while the word robots is the application or product of the robotic work. To make a robot function requires a combination of gears, sensors, controllers, hardware and software, creativity, computer programming, and mechanical aptitude. Machines that can be instructed to do a task are considered robots, whereas a machine that cannot be instructed to do a task is considered automata, from the Greek word for automatic.

Working in the field of robotics is exciting and getting more so every day. Because of technological leaps in the computer industry, many new opportunities are emerging. Engineers, programmers, and technicians design and maintain robots, research new applications for robots, and assist people in doing tasks that are less desirable. Robots have enormous potential for society. Equipped with the proper sensors, robots can inspect the quality of meat, measure the pollution emissions of manufacturing plants, assist in surgery, detect corrosion in sewer pipes, investigate the depths of a volcano, or assess the speed of a tornado. Robots can be used to improve the standard of living and provide more information about the planet as a whole, or even the solar system.

As a Roboticist, you might find yourself at work as a(n):
- Biomedical engineer designing tiny robots that can go inside the human body to destroy blood clots.
- Search and rescue engineer helping save lives after a hurricane or tsunami.
- Fire protection engineer creating a robot that can save people from burning buildings.
- Civil engineer searching for stress cracks on bridges or buildings.
- Ocean engineer using an underwater robot to search for buried treasure.
- Agricultural engineer designing ways to improve a harvest.
- Manufacturing engineer improving the safety in large manufacturing facilities.
- Transportation engineer creating robotic vehicles to shuttle people efficiently and safely.
- Explosive ordnance technician helping users of defense robots to stay out of harms way.
- Design engineer determining how to use robots to clean and organize our homes, and so much more!

Not all careers are discussed in this book and if of interest to you, should be investigated further.

The word robot was first coined by Czech playwright, Karel Capek, in his play, Rossum's Universal Robot, about humanlike machines. Robot comes from the Czech word robota, which means hard work or forced labor. The word "robot" entered the English language in 1923 when Rossum's Universal Robot, opened in London.

Who wouldn't want a robot to work hard and cook and clean for them? The robot would never complain nor get tired. Having a party for 50 of your closest friends? It is not a problem if you have a robot to clean the house before and after, to greet guests at the door, to serve drinks, and to ensure that the temperature, lighting, and music levels are just right throughout the night.

Engineers, technologists, programmers, and technicians are hard at work developing robots that can help alleviate some of the more time consuming chores around the house so you can do something more enjoyable. Robots in the home are currently being used to clean floors (e.g., vacuuming, scrubbing, and mopping), swimming pools, and windows. In addition, they can mow your lawn

Roomba Vacuum Cleaner by iRobot

and clean your gutters. Advances are being made in the design and development of ironing robots, intelligent refrigerators, and digital wardrobes. Smart homes—homes that are equipped with technology to maintain human comfort, convenience, security, and entertainment—are also on the rise. You can expect a future of more robotic devices helping in everyday life. Because robots have the potential to make home life easier, it's almost a surprise that the use of robots is not already integrated into all homes.

Robots most likely built the home appliances, such as the washing machine, refrigerator, and dishwasher you use every day. They locate items and package orders at mail order stores, such as Amazon.com. Underwater robots maintain pipelines so you can get gasoline for your car. Robots can do tasks that are highly repetitive, hazardous, dull, dirty, and dangerous.

Robots have been used primarily in the manufacturing industry, which continues to be the largest employer of robotic engineers. Automobiles are often built with the aid of a programmable machine that incorporates great precision, speed, and power. Robotics is also expanding to mining, agriculture, and other fields that are hazardous or undesirable to people. Robotic engineers work closely with computer programmers, electrical, mechanical, and manufacturing engineers, and production managers.

Who works in Robotics?

Robotics is a field that involves the use of many fields of technology. It's an industry that provides opportunities for endless creativity, innovation, and the pioneering of new ideas. People who work in robotics are engineers, computer programmers, designers, technologists, and technicians. Engineers and technologists will usually design a robot, incorporating sensors, gears, manipulators, cameras, power, and controllers. Computer programmers will write the code that gives the robot intelligence and technicians will build, install, and maintain the robot.

The good news is that if you are interested in robotics, you can study almost any type of engineering or technology. The most common engineering majors in addition to robotic engineering are biomedical, computer, electrical, electromechanical, mechanical, manufacturing, and software engineering. The opportunities in the study of robots and robotics are so broad that almost any field of interest can be combined with robotics, which creates a dream job.

Dr. Chris Jones, the Director of Strategic Development for iRobot says that robotics is an exciting and unique field.

"It requires tight integration of mechanical (e.g., motors, chassis, gears), electrical (e.g., processor, electronics, sensors) and software (e.g., take inputs, send commands, get the robot to do something) engineering concepts. Systems engineering is also a big part of getting the mechanical, electrical, and software to interact and play together. The best candidates for employment have depth in either mechanical, electrical, or software engineering and breadth in all. They understand the trade-offs and how the different parts of the robot might impact each other. They are able to cross boundaries between the fields. The best people may also have some experience with business and even psychology to understand how humans interact with machines. The user experience is critical to designing a robot that is well used by society."

There are many types of engineers, technologists, and technicians that work together to create a robot for a specific purpose. See more about the different types of engineering and engineering technology in *Part Four—The Many Approaches to Careers in Robotics*.

The engineers who work in robotics are usually:
- Biomedical engineers—apply robotics to improve healthcare
- Computer engineers—create the hardware and computer systems
- Electrical engineers—design the electronics of a robot
- Electromechanical engineers—make sure the electronics and hardware work together

- Industrial design engineers—design the look and form of a robot
- Manufacturing engineers—apply robotics to manufacturing systems
- Mechanical engineers—design the moving parts
- Robotics engineers—do a little of everything and put all the pieces together
- Software engineers—write the code that controls a robot
- Systems engineers—ensure a robot works as a system and whole

The technologists and technicians who work in robotics will have associates' or bachelors' degrees. They usually have degrees in:
- Biomedical Engineering Technology
- Computer Engineering Technology
- Electrical Engineering Technology
- Electromechanical Engineering Technology
- Manufacturing Engineering Technology
- Mechanical Engineering Technology

In this text:
- An engineer is defined as a person with a bachelor's or graduate degree in engineering
- An engineering technologist is defined as a person who has a bachelor's or graduate degree in any field of engineering technology
- An engineering technician is defined as a person who has an associate's degree or certificate of completion in any field of engineering technology

Engineers usually build a one of a kind or the first of a kind. The Space Shuttle was an engineering marvel and so was the first cell phone. But when cell phone manufacturers wanted to produce millions of phones a year, Engineering Technology (ET) became much more important. In many design scenarios, the engineer develops the "big picture" and the ET graduate fleshes out the details.

Because engineering is a constantly changing process, it is more of a journey than a destination. Engineers and technologists constantly strive to make things better. They may develop new sensors that are used to detect obstacles today, but they don't stop there. The next week, they may work on improving the onboard camera system, or have a new idea about how to include solar panels so robots can power themselves more efficiently.

Engineers are generally focused on a very specific area. They are using theory to improve or develop products, technologies, and systems. Technologists also design and develop products or technologies, which allow you to use the products and systems. Technologists may also work alongside engineers in research and development (R&D). When technologists work in R&D, they apply their ideas in the development of prototypes or to test existing research. Others work in quality control, inspecting products and processes, conducting tests, or collecting data. In manufacturing, technologists may work in product design, development, quality control, test engineering, sales, or production. They can be supervisors to connect the design professionals with the contractors or hourly workers.

It is important to realize that every machine has a designer, a builder, or fabricator, an installer, a maintainer, and someone who prepares the machine to be ready to do what it was designed to do. Engineers and technologists are usually the designers although the technologists may also build the machine, test it, support the design process led by an engineer, and get it ready to do what it is supposed to do. For example, technologists may develop the process settings in order that quality parts are produced from that machine. The technicians usually install, maintain, and program the machine. Another example is in the development of a new lamp. An engineer has the idea for a new lamp on paper. The technologist applies the engineer's idea and oversees how other aspects of the lamp relate to its manufacture and implementation. The technician would then review the practical applications of use and maintenance of the lamp.

ENGINEERS

Engineers are generally focused in one area of study, such as electrical, mechanical, computer, manufacturing, etc. Engineers are asked to understand why something occurs and to determine the theoretical understanding of a problem. An engineering education teaches the theoretical foundation of one specific area.

Engineers apply creativity, innovation, problem solving, mathematics, and analytical thinking to a project or a process they are designing or improving.

Advantages of an engineering degree include:
- Very rewarding to design products and/or processes that can save lives and benefit human-kind
- Understanding of high level mathematics gives greater understanding of the world around you, and application of this to real problems can be very satisfying
- Education is very broad and provides the foundation to continue schooling to become doctors, lawyers, writers, teachers, and business people
- Consistently excellent job opportunities at the bachelor's degree level
- Greater opportunity for advancement than an associate's degree
- Easier to continue to graduate school than engineering technology
- Engineers often escalate to management positions and earn more over the life of their careers
- Ease of the professional licensure process compared to technology degree holders
- Great salary right out of school and excellent earning potential throughout your lifetime

Disadvantages of an engineering degree include:
- The work can be stressful – especially when the work is associated with life and safety. For example, new medical

devices are built to specification, on time, and within budget. If something goes wrong with the design and it threatens the life or safety of a person, the engineer's job (and peace of mind) may hang in the balance. She/he could lose her or his Professional Engineering license for life.

- More time in school than an associate's degree (i.e., higher cost for college).
- Workload can be unpredictable and at times very high.
- Competitive atmosphere for promotion (i.e., performance as perceived by superiors determines one's ability to be promoted).
- Less diversity in training. Often, engineering students have very little opportunity to take business, manufacturing, art, or writing courses.
- Very rigorous and abstract mathematics is required - academic programs place a heavy emphasis on calculus, mathematics, and analytical work.

ENGINEERING TECHNOLOGISTS

The lines of separation between bachelor's level engineering and engineering technology positions in industry are blurring as the fields and responsibilities overlap more today than at any other time in history. Engineering Technology is a field that focuses on the application of established science, mathematics, engineering, and technology principles. A technologist is an expert at applying engineering principles and technology to solve problems and connect the theory to all aspects of a problem. An engineering technologist looks at the big picture and practical application of a problem. Both engineers and engineering technologists may design a product to solve a problem, but the engineer would be the one to discover new technology (e.g., microwaves) or develop new engineering principles and practices. The technologist would normally be the one to develop a product that uses the new technology (e.g., a microwave oven) as well as adapting, building, installing, and maintaining the new product or process. An engineer may design a product to solve a problem, but the technologist may develop the process to create that product quickly, inexpensively, and with high quality. Therefore, the technologist may be responsible for solving the problems that may occur during implementation.

With additional coursework, the technologist assists with the development and modification of a design in a broader aspect. The engineer has a very focused view of a product. Conversely, some engineers are also involved in the process design, but most of the time that is the work of a technologist.

Advantages of a bachelor's level engineering technology degree include:

- Work can be challenging and rewarding
- Employers appreciate the real-world problem-solving aspects of your education
- Numerous areas of study available
- Less engineering theory and more application-based education; Coursework may include real-world projects. You will be able to 'hit the ground running' in your career
- Some protection from out-sourcing of work to foreign countries due to the role in the building process of a machine or other product
- Consistent and excellent job opportunities worldwide
- May be hired as an engineer and compete with students with engineering degrees for jobs

Advantages of a bachelor's level engineering technology degree over an associate's degree include:

- Greater advancement opportunities than a technician
- Greater salary immediately upon graduation and more earning potential throughout the lifetime of the career
- Education of a technologist is very broad. Engineering technologists are able to take a wider variety of courses related to things, such as business and manufacturing depending on the discipline due to the number of

requirements for mathematics and science
- Engineering technologists frequently climb high on the management career ladder
- More mathematics and science can enable an easier transition into an engineering program, if desired

Disadvantages of a bachelor's level engineering technology degree (compared to an associate's program) include:
- More time in school resulting in higher cost for college
- Can be challenging to move into engineering fields or degree programs, due to higher mathematics requirements
- The work can be stressful
- May result in an inability to become a licensed engineer in some states despite successfully performing engineering design work—not all states will allow this degree to be professional engineers
- Job opportunities may be limited because some larger companies have a policy to only hire four-year engineering graduates
- May be performing similar work as an engineer, but not receive comparable recognition or compensation

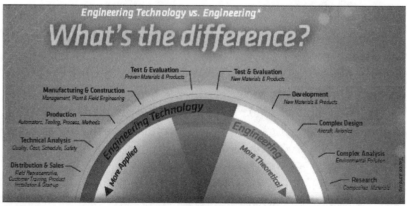

Program differences between bachelor of science programs in engineering technology and engineering. Reprinted with permission from the American Society of Mechanical Engineers (ASME) and Wichita State University.

ENGINEERING TECHNICIANS

Engineering technicians with an associate's degree focus on applying established engineering technology principles in applications, such as research and development, product design, manufacturing, and production processes. Engineering technicians work in research and development, build or set up equipment, prepare and conduct experiments, collect data, calculate or record results, conduct preliminary analysis, and help engineers or scientists in other ways, such as making prototype versions of newly designed equipment. They also assist in design work, often using Computer-Aided Design (CAD) or Computer-Aided Design and Drafting (CADD) equipment. The engineering technician is concerned with applying technology to install and maintain machines and to aid in the interfaces between systems and people.

An engineering technician is defined as a person who has an associate's degree or certificate of completion in any field of engineering technology. Some technicians are trained within military schools and many are trained within non-credit programs that may not include general education courses, such as English or humanities.

Advantages of an associate's engineering technology (ET) degree include:
- Generally less stress, and you can leave work behind at quitting time each day
- Since many fields have multiple technicians supporting one engineer the number of total jobs available is often greater for technicians than engineers
- ABET accredited programs offer credits that are transferable to a Bachelor of Science engineering technology program.
- More classes in major—all technical courses you take are relevant and there are minimal general education requirements needed

- Practical and applied mathematics and science—not as theoretical as engineering
- Abundant job opportunities worldwide and the jobs are not as vulnerable to outsourcing
- ET graduate is a preferred hire by many small, local companies where the job duties tend to be more varied and growth potential can be huge
- The work is hands-on and often does not require a technician to be stuck in an office or behind a desk
- Less time in school resulting in saving money
- Course work is usually offered at a nearby community college
- Great salary for only two to three years of school
- Sometimes companies pay for you to complete your bachelor's degree

Disadvantages of an associate's engineering technology degree include:
- More competition for jobs
- It's difficult to transition from a technician to an engineer because most of the time, the science classes in an associate's level engineering technology program are not calculus based, therefore science classes must be repeated. Some community colleges have ways to get around this disadvantage such as "two for one" articulation agreements and bridge courses
- There is less long-term flexibility in the career and less opportunity for advancement unless you seek advanced training
- Salary increases may get smaller over time if you do not seek advanced education or training to stay current in your job skills
- The work can be stressful or demanding depending on the project, but with less of the responsibility of an engineering technologist or engineer

How Do You Get into the Field of Robotics?

When you work with other people, good communication skills are necessary. Communication skills include the ability to listen, write clearly, and speak well. Rarely do people work alone. A roboticist must be able to tell others what is happening with a project, what to expect, and what is needed, verbally and in writing. In addition, they must be able to document all work, both to make it repeatable and for a potential patent or proof of intellectual property. Specifications, proposals, briefings, and reports are all part of the job. It is important to learn to communicate effectively—there is no downside to being a good communicator.

In addition to being good communicators, roboticists need to be passionate, energetic, creative, and excited about their work. The robotic industry is continually evolving and changing. It is important that in your preparation to enter the field of robotics that you take extra classes in technical writing, public speaking, and communications. You need to develop excellent presentation and speaking skills. In addition, it is important that you choose an industry that makes you excited about your career in order to commit yourself to being the best you can be. To succeed, focus your energy, meet your goals, pay attention to details, and allow time for creativity to evolve.

If you want to work in the robotics industry, the most valuable thing you can do is to get practical hands-on experience. Get involved. Take classes in electronics, and learn the basics from a technical viewpoint. Explore the practical knowledge (i.e., the nuts and bolts) of what you are learning, and then participate in as many different opportunities as you can to put that knowledge to work. If you go to work for a manufacturer, the experience will be invaluable to you. You want to learn how to relate to a customer who may use the products you design and you want to learn how to talk on that customer's level. This knowledge and your experiences will also be valuable to the manufacturer of the product you design. You will be able to share hands-on, practical information based on learning how customers use the products the manufacturer makes.

Academic preparation is essential in order to pursue robotics as a career. In addition to coursework, getting involved in extracurricular activities pertaining to robotics will give you valuable experience. In high school, classes in Algebra I and II, trigonometry, biology, physics, calculus, chemistry, and computer programming or computer applications will help you to determine if you have the aptitude and determination. Not all of these courses are required for acceptance into an engineering school, but early preparation will mean the difference between spending four years in college or six. For admission, some universities also require two to three classes in a foreign language. Check into the programs that interest you and begin to work toward fulfilling their requirements. For example, many programs of study in robotics recommend future applicants take Advance Placement (AP) or Honors courses as well as to read and study in order to acquire an ACT score of 20 or a SAT score of at least 1000.

Part II–Types of Robots

Robots either move or they don't.

Robots that stay in one place are referred to as fixed robots. They are generally used in manufacturing and consist of an arm with an elbow joint (or several) and a hand or end-effector. Fixed robots perform repetitive tasks over a small area.

The type of robot used in any situation is largely determined by the needs of that particular situation. In a factory, robots may be stationary or fixed in place if the task to be accomplished is within a small area, such as packing products in a box. The robot will be mobile if travel is required, such as searching for survivors after a hurricane or other natural disaster.

Fixed Robots–Factory and Industrial Manipulators

Industrial robots are fixed in place with the exception of KIVA (*See page 30*). An industrial robot is an automatically controlled, reprogrammable, multipurpose manipulator that is programmable in three or more axes. In other words, the robot is stationary, but can move its arm up, down, in, out and sideways (i.e., through all three of the x-, y-, and z-axis) due to its programming. This enables the industrial robot to complete specific tasks. The end-effectors can have as many as three wrist movements for yaw (side to side), pitch (up and down), and rotational (clockwise and counterclockwise) movement.

Industrial roboticists study, design, and use robots and robotic systems in manufacturing and other industries. These robots are usually designed to perform tasks, such as welding, painting, assembly, packaging, product inspection, and testing. The benefit of having robots do these tasks is that they have high endurance, never get bored, can lift heavy parts, are fast, precise, often work in the dark (i.e., without lights) and don't require the same climate conditions as people.

Industrial robots consist of an arm, elbow joint, and an end effector. The end effector is one of the most essential parts of an

industrial robot and is similar to a hand, but designed to hold one type of object or perform one task. End effectors can be swapped out, which enables a programmed

Packaging Robot

robot to perform different tasks. Common examples of end effectors include welding devices (e.g., MIG-welding guns, spot-welders), spray guns, grinding and deburring devices (e.g., pneumatic disks or belt grinders, burrs), and grippers, which are devices that can grasp an object, usually electromechanical or pneumatic. Another common way robots are programmed to pick up objects is through the use of a vacuum. End effectors are complex, customized to match the task at hand, and often capable of picking up many items or products at one time. They may use a multitude of sensors to help a robotic system locate, handle, and position the items or products for the next task.

Industrial robots are exceptional for doing work that is exhausting, harmful, dangerous, or boring for people. Usually, a robot is programmed to do one repetitive task endlessly. They can work around the clock and never tire. These robots don't think. There is no intelligence built in, which means they cannot correct errors. For example, if an industrial robot's job is to paint cars, it can't see or visualize. It has no way to detect if a car is actually in front of it, or if the car is ready to be painted. The industrial robot also does not know if the sensor stating the car is in the ready position is faulty or if the car has already been painted and the conveyor belt is stuck. All the robot knows is that it is supposed to shoot paint in a specific pattern at a specific point and time. There are sensors inside the robot to tell it if the paint bucket is empty or if the spray gun is clogged, but it has no external sensors to let it know if the car is present or if there are people standing in the way. Industrial robots have the potential to be dangerous to humans because the robots have no means to stop their work, intelligently or independently, even if injury has occurred—with the exception of Baxter (*See page 31*).

The most commonly used robot configurations are articulated robots, SCARA robots, delta robots, and Cartesian coordinate robots, also called gantry robots or x-y-z robots. In the context of general robotics, most types would be categorized as robotic arms.

Robots exhibit varying degrees of autonomy:
- Some robots are programmed to faithfully carry out specific actions repeatedly (i.e., repetitive actions) without variation and with a high degree of accuracy. These actions are determined by programmed routines that specify the direction, acceleration, velocity, deceleration, and distance of a series of coordinated motions.
- Other robots are much more flexible as to the orientation of the object on which they are operating or even the task that has to be performed on the object itself, which the robot may even need to identify. For example, for more precise guidance, robots often contain machine vision sub-systems acting as their visual sensors, linked to powerful computers or controllers. Artificial intelligence,

or what passes for it, is becoming an increasingly important factor in the modern industrial robot.

Source: Industrial robot. (2015, February 8). In Wikipedia, The Free Encyclopedia. Retrieved 15:38, February 13, 2015, from http://en.wikipedia.org/w/index.php?title=Industrial_robot&oldid=646121529

According to the International Federation of Robotics (IFR) the number of operational industrial robots is estimated to reach 1,575,000 by the end of 2015. There are more industrial robots than any other type of robot. These robots allow manufacturing companies to be highly productive, produce consistent quality, and are adaptable at a minimal cost. The biggest use (60%) of industrial robots is in the automotive industry. Robots can be very precise with a skilled programmer. They are commonly used in manufacturing processes that include gluing, precision assembly, painting, welding, machining, and coating, to name a few. High-growth industries, such as electronics, food, and retail packaging in large companies, such as Amazon.com also use advanced robot technology. The advanced robots are programmed to safely handle chemicals and lift and maneuver heavy objects, such as sheets or rolls of metal.

The one exception to the historical fact that all industrial robots are fixed in place is the advent of Amazon.com's Kiva robot in 2014. The Kiva robots, essentially smart forklifts, are designed to help workers while they work in warehouses. Kiva robots are programmed to bring inventory to the workers instead of making the workers walk around a large warehouse looking for the inventory. The benefits add up quickly when 1,000 Kiva robots or more are used in each of the seventy Amazon.com warehouses. A central computer keeps track of each robot preventing run-ins as the robots buzz around the warehouse floor.

SAFETY IN INDUSTRIAL ROBOTS

Without safety checks in place, a robot could do a lot of damage. An industrial robot does not have the intelligence to assess a situation and stop what it is doing. Robots are programmed complete a single task and have no sensors to detect what anything else or anyone else is doing at the same time. The fixed industrial robot is fast, powerful, and its arm can move over large area. Examples of when a potential safety hazard may occur:

- During the changing of the programmed movements of a robot when an object's work order is changed or is moved.
- While working in close proximity of two or more robots, which requires understanding the dangers. For example, if a robot goes haywire, a worker could be hit by one robot while working on another, trapped between the two robots or other equipment, or hit with flying objects.

For these reasons, 'fixed robots' are most often placed in caged areas to keep humans out when the robots are working.

Baxter, made by ReThink, was the first robot built as an exception to this rule. Baxter was designed to improve workplace safety. Its adaptability made it ideal for working next to people. Baxter robots are able to multi task and can be moved around the factory to new work sites in-lieu of moving the work to the robot.

Baxter Robot

Most robot accidents do not happen under normal operating conditions. It's very rare for operators to be injured by robots. This may be due in part to the safety constraints put into place. It's more common that human injuries happen during programming, re-programming, maintenance, repair, testing, setup, or adjustment. This is because the maintenance and testing of a robot often requires moving within the robot's working space. This would place the operator, programmer, or technician temporarily in a location that could result in injury.

The expected hazards are most often due to human errors, control errors, unauthorized access, mechanical failures, environmental sources, power systems, and improper installation. Roboticists of all types are needed to improve the design and capabilities of industrial robots as well as the safety systems that prevent injury. Every type of engineer, technologist, and technician can help increase the diversity of applications robots can be designed to perform. As a result, versions of these robots will be brought into more businesses and homes of the future. Perhaps an industrial robot, working inside your refrigerator, will someday pack your lunch each morning. The time and work-saving opportunities created by the designs of robots of the future are limited only by your imagination.

Mobile Robots

If the base of a robot moves, it is considered a mobile robot. Mobile robots may be built with wheels, pulleys, wings, rotors, fins, or feet. They can slither like snakes, pop out of walls to extinguish fires, sense light and noise, taste for hazardous chemicals, run like a cheetah, clean up hazards, check in with football players after injuries, pack and ship items, and more. Mobile robots are everywhere. As you read along, you'll learn about many of their applications.

Robots that move are referred to as mobile robots and generally fall into three categories. They can be:

1. Ground vehicles—Manned and unmanned. A ground vehicle usually consists of a robot, a control system, and an operator. The robot can be on a tether that supplies power and operation commands with instructions or operated wirelessly. A wireless vehicle will require its own battery and will sometimes be larger because of it.

2. Aerial vehicles—These may also be called aerial systems, remotely piloted vehicles, or Unmanned Aerial Vehicles (UAVs). Aerial vehicles can be fixed wing, such as a plane or jet or incorporate vertical takeoff and landing, such as a helicopter.

3. Marine vehicles— Vehicles that perform tasks on the surface or underwater.

GROUND ROBOTS

Ground robots can be manned or unmanned. Unmanned are often referred to as UGVs (i.e., Unmanned Ground Vehicles) where no one is riding in the robot like in the case of a rover robot on Mars or a Roomba robot vacuuming your floors. A manned vehicle doesn't necessarily mean a man is operating the robot but rather a terminology used in industry to say that  someone is riding in the robot like in the case of an agricultural robot plowing a field by GPS or satellite navigation.

A ground robot is the most common type of mobile robot. It usually consists of a robot, which is considered the hardware; a control system (i.e., the software); and an operator. The robot operates on the ground as opposed to in the air or in the water. The robot can be on a tether that supplies power and operation commands with instructions or it may be operated wirelessly. A wireless vehicle will require its own battery, which may make it heavier and larger.

Ground robots are divided into three size categories:
- Maxi—large robots that go into the same spaces as humans. They are heavy and cumbersome, but extremely useful in agriculture, construction, mining, and chemically hazardous situations.
- Portable—mid-sized robots that are about the size of a small person. They can be carried to a work location and are often found in hospitals, and packing and shipping companies, such as Amazon.com, and are the most common robots depicted in movies and entertainment.
- Packable—small robots that are easy to carry and can explore areas that humans and dogs cannot fit or that are not safe for either. Packable robots are commonly used to find survivors after hurricanes, tsunamis, earthquakes, and other natural or human-made disasters as well as explosive ordnance disposal.

If a robot that moves on the ground can assist a person, it can be considered a mobile ground robot. Ground robots are used in search and rescue where they gain access to areas that humans and dogs cannot fit. In

Soldier carrying a packable robot

space exploration, ground robots are used to explore planets that do not support human life. The agriculture and forestry industries use robots, which allow farmers to plant and harvest a larger area. In mining, ground robots help to increase productivity and provide for the health and safety of mining workers. Preventing injury in hazardous applications, such as bomb sniffing helps to protect law enforcement during conflicts and criminal activities.

If you are interested in a career in the mobile ground robot industry, there are tremendous opportunities. Roboticists are needed to:

1. Stabilize and improve robotic cameras so that pictures are clear and high quality. In a search and rescue mission, the ability to enhance and enlarge photos is a critical benefit.
2. Improve the interface between the operator and the robot to increase safety and reduce errors.
3. Improve mobility for different terrains or situations. A firefighting robot needs multiple forms of mobility because it may need to step over obstacles, go up or down a flight of stairs, or hang on a wall to get a better vantage point.
4. Improve sensors and data processing algorithms so that the robot doesn't collide with objects in its path, such as people, other robots, and roadblocks.

Engineers and technologists interested in ground robots, vehicles, and exploration technology may find opportunities as a(n):

- Robotic Engineer, who develops the robot power systems and works with other engineers to integrate all the systems together in any ground vehicle.
- Computer Engineer, who develops the hardware for the robot's control system.
- Electrical Engineer, who may develop the electrical systems and technology to generate, store, or distribute the energy to the robot. They may be responsible for battery systems, wireless cameras, computer and

communications systems, sensors, underwater lighting, and the logistics of collecting data.

- Mechanical Engineer, who may design the generators or power systems for ground robots and vehicles. They may build and test prototypes, make CAD models, or write and apply for patents.
- Environmental Engineer, who participates in the design of a robot to protect people and the environment by limiting toxic materials, and they assess the processes used during construction of the robot.
- Software Engineer, who works with computer engineers to design the controls for every system in a robot.

AERIAL ROBOTS

The existence of aerial robots has been dated back to Leonardo da Vinci. In the early days of flight, aerial robots may have been developed in order to keep a pilot safe while refinements to the stability, construction, and controls were made to an aircraft.

A large number of potential applications exist for robots that have the advantages offered through flight. The U.S. Federal Aviation Administration (FAA) has adopted the name Unmanned Aircraft (UA) to describe aircraft systems without a flight crew on board. Names that are more common include Unmanned Aerial Vehicle (UAV), drone, Remotely Piloted

Vehicle (RPV), Remotely Piloted Aircraft (RPA), and Remotely Operated Aircraft (ROA). They can be fixed wing (e.g., a plane or jet) or rotary wing with the capability of a vertical takeoff and landing (e.g., a helicopter).

UAs are usually tele-operated (i.e., untethered) with a remote control type of device. They are largely autonomous, but are also controlled by a remote operator and subject to civil regulations. Using GPS-enabled satellite navigation with an autopilot, a UA can fly up or down, go to a given destination, and land, and then take off again. They typically need very little input from a remote pilot. This means that the pilot can focus on the robot's status, position, and on the purpose of the flight.

UAs can be used to take pictures, forecast the weather, measure the temperature of sea ice in Alaska, collect meteorological data, monitor traffic congestion, inspect bridges and other waterline structures, communicate for disaster response, and provide for the transportation and delivery of goods. UAs are also used to find humans lost in the wilderness, in collapsed buildings, or adrift at sea. The military often refers to UAs as drones, which have been used since the beginnings of powered flight.

According to Eric Feron and Eric Johnson in the book, *Springer Handbook of Robotics*, the applications of Aerial Robotics falls into nine categories.

1. Remote Sensing, such as pipeline spotting, power line monitoring, volcanic sampling, mapping, meteorology, geology, and agriculture as well as unexploded mine detection.
2. Disaster response, such as chemical sensing, flood monitoring and wildfire management.
3. Surveillance, such as law enforcement, traffic monitoring, coastal and maritime patrol, and border patrol.
4. Search and Rescue in low-density or hard-to-reach areas.
5. Transportation, which includes small and large cargo transport and possible passenger transport.

6. Communications as permanent or ad hoc relays for voice and data transmission as well as broadcast units for television or radio.
7. Payload delivery, such as used for firefighting or crop dusting.
8. Image acquisition, such as used for cinematography or real-time entertainment.
9. Military applications with a particular emphasis on remote sensing of humans and critical infrastructure, surveillance of human activity, payload delivery (e.g., bombs, missiles), and ad hoc ground infrastructures devoted to communication and surveillance.

The popularity of unmanned aerial robots is increasing. In recent years, the word drone has taken on a more common use. Improvements in flight controls, cameras systems, and communications has provided views from angles not easily seen and have saved time and resources by providing images on demand, allowed more exploration of the solar system, and facilitated in the structural inspection of bridges and buildings with the capability of hovering as close as six to seven feet from a structure.

If you are interested in a career in the UA industry, there are tremendous opportunities. Roboticists are needed to:
1. Stabilize and improve the onboard cameras for clear and high-quality images. The cameras need to be designed to take images even in turbulence and at high speed. The cameras also need to pan and tilt independently of the UA. A UA with a fixed camera hinders and slows its exploration because the UA needs to turns the entire aircraft to capture an image.
2. Improve the communication abilities between a pilot operator and the UA to improve safety and reduce errors.
3. Improve takeoffs, landings, and dockings with other vehicles. UAs can be used to refuel planes in the air, but

not without improving the coordination and physical interaction between vehicles.

4. Improve the onboard sensors to avoid obstacles to prevent the UA from colliding with other aircraft, buildings, wind turbines, suspended cables, and birds. There is a need for research and development of sensors, sensors management systems, and data processing algorithms to instruct an UA to get out of the way of potential obstacles.

Engineers and technologists interested in aerial robots and vehicles and exploration technology may find opportunities as an:

- Aerospace/Aeronautical Engineer that would develop the propulsion systems and work with other engineers to integrate all the systems together in any aerial vehicle.
- Computer Engineer that develops the hardware for a robot's control system.
- Electrical Engineer that might develop the electrical systems and technology to generate, store, or distribute the energy to an aerial vehicle. They may be responsible for battery systems, wireless cameras, computer and communications systems, sensors, aerial lighting, and the logistics of collecting data.
- Environmental Engineer that designs methods to protect people and the environment through limiting toxic materials. They assess the processes used during construction of a robot or aircraft.
- Mechanical Engineer that may design the generators or power systems for aerial robots and vehicles. They may build and test prototypes, make CAD models, or write and apply for patents.
- Software Engineer that works with computer engineers to design the controls for every system involved within and on a UA robot.

MARINE ROBOTS

The oceans hold many mysteries, and people have always wanted and tried to explore them. Finding new species of fish or other aquatic organisms, studying the bottom of the ocean, and investigating new forms of life are just a few examples of ocean exploration. What's down there? Ships have sunk and treasure hunters have lined up to look for loot. Historians stand in awe at the artifacts that have been brought up to the surface after sunken ships, such as the Titanic have been discovered. These artifacts enable historians to have a snapshot of what life might have been like in the past.

For more than 2000 years, people have worked underwater and explored the seas. From Alexander the Great to the Japanese and Korean pearl divers to Jacques Cousteau and many others, finding ways to explore the oceans has interested some of the greatest minds in history. Humans, with fragile bodies, cannot live in water without the aid of technology. Some of this technology has been invented, but more engineering is required that will enable humans to explore the vast bodies of water on Earth.

To explore the ocean, engineers have invented many different types of vehicles. In the early 1700s, John Lethbridge made a diving chamber that was a waterproof wooden barrel with holes cut out for arms and for visibility. It was lowered from a boat with a rope to a maximum depth of sixty-five feet. In this rudimentary diving chamber, he successfully salvaged shipwreck treasures and artifacts from the ocean floor.

Humans wanted to explore deeper, but not while in wooden barrels. In the 1800s, the first submarine was designed and constructed in France by Robert Fulton. It was twenty-five feet long, powered by hand, and had a mast and sail for use while it was on the surface of the water.

By the late 1800s, the U.S. Navy bought its first submarine, which was developed by John Holland and used in World Wars I and II. It had an electric motor for underwater propulsion and a gasoline motor to travel on the surface. Surface travel also allowed for the recharging of its batteries, a benefit during long trips.

These designs and many others have been improved because of engineering and technological advancements. There are four main types of underwater robot vehicles.

1.   Remotely Operated Vehicle (ROV) - ROVs are underwater robots that are operated with a cable or tether. They can be any shape or size, and are usually designed for a specific job. Underwater ROVs search for treasure or artifacts, facilitate researching and studying the lives of sea creatures, salvaging materials from the ocean floor, and maintaining oil rigs or other underwater structures. Usually, a ROV is unmanned—meaning that no human is riding in or on the robot.

The ROV operator uses a hand-held control device, similar to a video game controller. The control device is used to provide commands and power (i.e., electricity) to the robot. The advantage of this system is that the ROV does not need an on-board battery, and if a video camera is attached, the footage can be seen in real time. The disadvantage is that the tether may hang on obstructions that are not seen with the onboard cameras. When searching for people or possessions after a hurricane or other serious storm, sea life can grow very fast and obscure the view. In such cases, the ROV is able to use sonar and topographical maps to detect people or items that are not visible.

Remotely Operated Vehicle (ROV)

The majority of devices in this category are considered "free swimming". With the help of an operator, the ROV can swim in any direction as well as crawl along the bottom. Other ROVs are towed by boats or dragged along the ocean floor to dig trenches for underwater cables or fiber-optic Internet lines. Some work more as tractors that crawl on the bottom of the ocean in very deep waters, and some facilitate research on underwater structures, such as oil rigs.

2. Autonomous Underwater Vehicle (AUV)—Autonomous means that the underwater robot can be operated without a tether. These robots swap the tether for wireless or Bluetooth communication. Similar to the ROV, they can be operated by one or more persons using a videogame-like controller directly or by a computer that has been programmed to give it specific commands.

    Like most autonomous vehicles, AUVs can be fully equipped with sonar and sensors to detect depth, obstacles, currents, and temperature that help to navigate the AUV and perform specific tasks. Being untethered, the AUV can explore underneath structures, shipwrecks, pollution, or ice patches in the Arctic regions.

It is expected that the AUV will become the most common robot for underwater exploration once the longevity of the battery technology improves the use of underwater Wi-Fi or Bluetooth. This improvement will enable large quantities of data to be collected during the period of submersion.

Autonomous Underwater Vehicle (AUV)

The current disadvantage to using AUVs is that the wireless connections underwater often do not work. The robot has to be programmed ahead of time to perform a specific operation with little or no knowledge of the environment because there is no camera providing real-time information. Power sources and cameras weigh an AUV down. This makes it impractical for an AUV to be used for long periods in order to uncover information about the ocean and what lies within.

Another problem encountered when using an AUV is drift. Without being able to "see" in real-time, currents can carry a robot far from its intended destination. On the ground, if a robot is told to stop, it stays in one place. In the water, when a robot is told to stop, the motor may stop, but a robot will drift.

3. Autonomous Surface Vehicles, or SUVs, use wireless communication to inspect bridges and other structures on the surface of water. The problem is that interference from the bridge structure or shadows caused by the bridge structure interfere with GPS communications. In the case of inspecting a bridge, a ROV may be a better choice, but it is more difficult to maneuver around pilings.

4. Manned Submersibles - Don't let the name mislead you—a manned vehicle can be manned or operated by a woman! Just as the term implies, manned submersibles are underwater vehicles that have one to three people onboard. It can be tethered or untethered, and only differs from a submarine in that a submarine is usually larger, has a crew of people onboard, and is used for tourism or military operations. This smaller submersible is considered a hybrid system, as it is usually equipped with robotic arms. Typically, it is used to do research, fix oil rigs, give tours, or perform salvage operations.

Engineers and technologists interested in underwater robots, vehicles, and exploration technology may find opportunities as an:

- Ocean Engineer that works both on and below the surface of the sea, studying ocean movements and their effect on the habitat both above and below the waterline. Ocean engineers may also be responsible for developing underwater tools and devices that aid underwater research.
- Electrical Engineer that may develop the electrical systems and technology to generate, store, or distribute the energy to underwater vehicles. They may be responsible for battery systems, wired and wireless cameras, waterproof computers, sensors, underwater lighting, and the logistics of collecting data.
- Mechanical Engineer that may design turbines, generators, or control systems for underwater robots and vehicles. They may build and test prototypes, make CAD models, or write and apply for patents.
- Civil Engineer that may design the mooring systems for any structure that needs to be anchored to the ocean floor either temporarily or permanently. They make sure that the attachments can sustain hurricanes, corrosion, and water pressure.
- Marine Engineer that develops the propulsion systems and works with other engineers to integrate all the systems together in any powered vehicle.

PART THREE—ROBOTIC APPLICATIONS

Robots in the Military

In 2012, a fire broke out on a nuclear submarine and injured seven people. During a fire on the USS Miami, sailors couldn't locate the source of the fire because the smoke was too thick. On a Destroyer ship at sea, twelve sailors suffered extensive burns when attempting to put out an engine-room fire.

The interiors of ships and submarines are small spaces that require agile and physically fit sailors. Some vessels have as many as four hundred sailors working aboard. When a fire breaks out, there is not enough space for hundreds to get out quickly and safely. Furthermore, when on the ocean, there may be nowhere to go. The fire must be extinguished quickly and efficiently.

Robots can help.

In 2014, the Office of Naval Research began testing robotic firefighters. Designed for high-risk applications, robots can go into intensely hot and smoky spaces, use advanced sensors  to see through the smoke, find doorways and the source of the flames, pick up, and then drag hoses to put out a fire, and locate victims.

The Navy spends billions of dollars on advanced technology, including robots, sophisticated equipment, and highly skilled engineers, technicians, and managers. Its mission is to maintain the freedom of the seas and to protect U.S. interests and those of U.S. allies around the world. When the Navy considers a robot, it must be able to balance and maneuver on a boat, see where it needs to go, and work autonomously. If a robot can detect a fire within minutes or seconds of it starting, many disasters and injuries can be avoided.

The roboticist who specializes in firefighting and works in this area of expertise for the Navy has many options, but must work within constraints. Ships and submarines typically have narrow doorways, hallways, and stairs. A robot with legs instead of wheels may be a good option. Or, a roboticist may design a small flying helicopter robot that can dump fire-extinguishing materials, locate the flames, and search for victims. Robots may be mounted to the walls throughout a vessel to autonomously aim and shoot water at a fire from short nozzles that are also attached to the wall. These are just a few of the possible design ideas that would be employed to protect those living on ships and submarines, and they are only the beginning of what is possible for a roboticist to design.

An important aspect that must be considered when designing a robot firefighter is that it needs to work autonomously—it can think on its own, understand the goal of extinguishing a fire safely, and make decisions. If a fire is detected, it must be smart enough to avoid spraying with water or dousing chemicals on the crew as it tries to put out a fire. Decision making intelligence must be built into the robot because it is unlikely that a person will be able to control it in an emergency. A couple of questions the designer needs to consider and be able to answer are: How will the robot know when the fire is extinguished completely? What if there are multiple fires onboard? Communication and teamwork with sailors is important—just as real firefighters work together. These issues and more ensure a bright future for using creative design in the development of military robots for robotic engineers, computer scientists, and researchers.

Another interest to the military is the use of robots to save lives. Research is currently being conducted to improve how robots can be used in dangerous situations to detect enemies and landmines, defuse Improvised Explosive Devices (IEDs), and carry wounded soldiers and heavy loads, such as water, ammo, and protective gear. Using real-time surveillance cameras, robots can send photos, videos, thermal imaging (i.e., heat maps) and other useful data to command centers and thereby keep soldiers out of harm's way. For the military, sending a robot in first is a way to help keep troops a safe distance from potential danger. For those soldiers, and likewise other safety personnel, such as bomb squads and police officers, the robot becomes a valuable partner upon which their life may depend.

Robot checking for IEDs

Scott Hartley, a senior research engineer and co-founder of 5D Robotics, said that he estimates that in ten years, there may be ten robots for every soldier in the U.S. military. He predicts that the robots will do everything from moving supplies around military bases to doing security patrols, following soldiers onto a battlefield, and even flanking soldiers during dangerous situations.

Another use of robotics that can benefit the military is minimizing soldier fatigue and reducing musculoskeletal injuries, which is one of the most common reasons for discharge from the military. The Wyss Institute for Biologically Inspired Engineering at Harvard University was awarded a contract from the Defense Advanced Research Projects Agency (DARPA) to develop further a biologically inspired smart suit. The suit will be designed to mimic the action of the leg muscles and tendons when a person walks, and will provide small but carefully timed assistance at the joints of the leg without restricting a wearer's movement.

The device, the Soft Exosuit, when completed will make moving easier. It will be worn under clothing and can enable soldiers to walk longer distances, without getting as tired, and reduce the risk of injury when carrying heavy loads. Essentially, it will be smart clothing that is pulled on like a pair of pants and worn under a soldier's regular gear. The suit will have flexible power systems, soft sensors, and controllers that enable intuitive and seamless human-machine interaction. The suit will have the capability to continuously monitor various data signals, including the suit tension, the position of the wearer (e.g., walking, running, crouched), and more.

In addition to its military application, the Soft Exosuit design team will collaborate with clinical partners to develop a medical version of the suit that will be able to help stroke patients that often experience a slow, inefficient gait and would greatly benefit from walking assistance.

Robots in Medicine and Healthcare

Medical robots, robot surgery, and other robotic technology that are designed to improve healthcare, save patients from pain, and at the same time, provide doctors with powerful tools for treating patients is on the rise. Robots in hospitals may help move and transfer patients from a bed to a couch or an operating table. They are used to serve as an automated transport system for drugs, assist disabled or elderly people (e.g., a robot walker can contribute to keeping an elderly person upright), or a robotic prosthesis (e.g., a robotic hand or arm can help a disabled person in daily life tasks). New robots in such areas as rehabilitation and health care are expected to improve quality of life for an aging population.

A robot may be used as a medical or paramedical personal assistant. Used in this way, a robot can take dictation during patient consultations, help patients to learn how to walk after spinal cord injuries, and are used as a patient-doctor communication interface. As mentioned in the section on *Robots in the Military*, an exoskeleton similar to an Exosuit is being developed for military applications. In addition, it could be used during rehabilitation with a patient who has suffered a stroke.

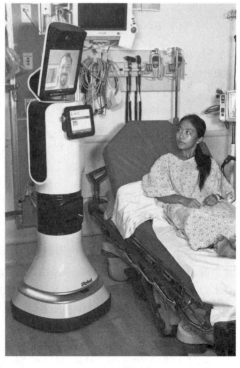

A robot may also provide a way for a doctor to see a patient remotely, extending the ability to care for patients beyond geographic bounds. Using video conferencing, a doctor in San Francisco can log into a robot that is physically located in a small rural town or remote area where a doctor is not readily available, and then remotely direct the robot to a patient's bedside for long distance diagnosis. This can save valuable time for patients in distress. For example, when a person has a stroke, every minute counts. A robot that enables a doctor to prescribe a treatment right away may make the difference between that person having permanent damage or not. Concerning the more instrumental side of medicine, robots can hold the "tool" required by the surgeon, radiologist, oncologist, or other surgeon during surgery or when performing a diagnostic or therapeutic assessment. For example, the robot could perform the machining of a bone cavity for a prosthetic limb, or carry and move a surgical microscope for microsurgery, an endoscope for minimally invasive surgery, or a linear accelerator for radiation therapy. A traditional surgical instrument could be designed to work as a robot that when placed in the right position, could perform a routine surgery on its own.

ROBOTIC SURGERY

One of the most interesting and promising developments in the field of medical technology is robotic surgery.

Simply stated, robotic surgery (also known as computer - assisted surgery or robotically assisted surgery) involves the use of advanced technological tools to assist surgeons in performing delicate surgical procedures, both with greater precision and with less stress on a patient's body. This type of surgical techniques is proving to work better than ordinarily achieved with traditional methods.

Surgery is interactive. A surgeon makes many decisions because of feedback from monitors and the patient in an operating room. Generally, the goal of surgical robotics is to improve a surgeon's ability to treat patients not to replace him or her. The robot is like a surgical assistant that a surgeon will use to improve the precision and outcome of a surgery. Robotic surgery may be broken into two subcategories:

1. Surgeon extender or tele-operated robots: These types of robots are used to manipulate surgical instruments under the direct control of a surgeon. In this scenario, a doctor in France can operate on a person in Boston. These

systems use software that can eliminate hand tremors in surgeons and help a patient recover quickly. This is also referred to as telemedicine.

2. Auxiliary Surgical Support Robots: These robots usually work in an operating room alongside a surgeon. The robots are used to perform routine tasks, as directed by the surgeon, such as drawing back tissue to expose parts of the body for surgery, holding limbs in a specific position, or holding equipment, such as endoscopes or laparoscopic instruments. This type of robot can speed procedures, reduce the number of people in an operating room, and as a result, decrease patient recovery time.

The potential benefits robotic surgery offers patients include shortened hospital stays, reduced pain, reduced loss of blood, reduced risk of infection, reduced scarring, and faster healing, resulting in a quicker return to normal activities. Further, the enhanced surgical precision a skilled surgeon can achieve using robotic surgical techniques reduce the risks of accidental damage to healthy tissues during operations—a factor that could raise patient confidence.

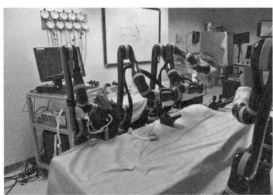
Robotic operating table

The first generation of surgical robots is already installed in a number of operating rooms around the world. For more than two decades, robots have been part of hospitals and have progressively become a common tool for a clinician. Robotics is being introduced to medicine because it allows for amazing control and precision of surgical instruments in minimally invasive procedures. For example, by using robots in surgery, only small incisions (i.e., .1-1.0 inches) need to be made to insert instruments and viewing equipment into the body, in contrast to open surgery with large incisions. This minimizes surgical trauma and damage to healthy tissue, resulting in shorter patient recovery time. Robots have been used to position an endoscope, navigate the vascular system, knee and hip surgery, eye repair, to perform gallbladder surgery, and correct acid reflux and heartburn. Work is underway to design a robot that can be used to perform heart surgery while the chest is closed as opposed to open-heart surgery. The ultimate goal of the robotic surgery field is to design robots that perform surgery in the least disruptive manner possible for the patient with the greatest accuracy and speed imaginable for the physician.

The use of robotics in surgery will expand over the next decades as advances are made and more technology and engineering solutions are found to address surgical problems and challenges.

The advantages of medical robots can be grouped into three areas:
1. Improve surgeons' technical capability, such as reducing hand tremors and allowing for more efficiency
2. Promote surgical safety
3. Promote consistency while capturing and recording the surgery itself

ROBOTIC INTERVENTION

Robotic intervention is another form of surgery. Unlike a physician performing surgery where the skin is cut to access the problem, in robotic intervention, physicians use X-Ray (fluoroscopy), MR (magnetic resonance), and sometimes ultrasonic probes that are small enough to fit inside the incision.

These small devices enable the surgeon to see inside the body and to guide a snake-like device through arteries to explore, remove, or repair the problem from the inside without making a large incision. Using this method, also known as minimally invasive surgery, the incision is very small (i.e., 1-20 mm), which means that there is less damage to surrounding tissue, less discomfort for the patient, and recovery times are typically shorter. This is a preferred method for many types of surgery and for treating patients who are not healthy enough for surgery. However, this procedure can be more challenging due to the indirect route required to access a problem within the body.

To perform interventional procedures, physicians will use guide wires and catheters to access and navigate the twisty path of the blood stream. These devices are long hollow channels that allow access for a physician's tiny tools. Surgeons watch images provided by fluoroscopy on a screen, and then direct the robotic hand, powered by electronic, hydraulic, or mechanical means to move to the desired location.

Typically, if a physician performs this surgery without the aid of a robot, he or she will navigate to the desired location by pushing, twisting, and turning the back of the device in hopes that

Micro-forceps for laparoscopic surgery.

the front end move where directed. With robotic intervention, a robotic device helps overcome the challenges of navigation and precision. It will steer directly where commanded without having to use specialized techniques and luck. Not only does this facilitate rapid navigation, it is also less stressful on the patient, and allows for pinpoint accuracy. Accuracy is very important since most catheters need to be within one mm of a lesion to properly administer therapy.

The different categories of robotic intervention devices include:

1. Assisted access: This includes those robots that can navigate the vascular system through the ability to directly steer catheters.

2. Therapy treatment: This includes the robotic administration of treatment. Treatment could include the robotic positioning of a stent or a valve, pinpoint administration of cancer treating drugs, or localized ablation of fibrillating muscle tissue or misfiring nerves.

While some of the robots may perform actions in both categories, many devices are designed specifically for access or treatment. All of the robots are designed to excel in one or more of the following aspects of a procedure:

1. Speed—The faster the procedure can be completed, the shorter the time necessary for the use of x-rays.

2. Precision—Greater accuracy will allow for faster treatment and reduce risk of a poorly performed procedure.

3. Simplification—Some interventional procedures, like surgical procedures, require the use of many tools and sometimes this means the use of several doctors. A robot will allow for one physician to control many tools.

4. Increased capability—Some robotic medical devices are so revolutionary, they enable doctors to provide treatments that were not possible before.

INTERVIEW WITH JOE BOGUSKY, STAFF R&D ENGINEER FOR
AURIS SURGICAL ROBOTICS

CB. How did you become interested in robotics?

Joe: I graduated with a degree in biomedical engineering and was working for a medical device company. During the assembly of some medical devices, automation equipment is frequently used for tasks that are repetitive; yet need to be very precise. For business reasons, the company wanted to find robotic solutions to help manufacturing personnel make its products more efficiently. I became extremely interested in and excited by the use of precision and repeatability and the seemingly infinite ways in which robots are used to improve work, play, and life.

CB: Did you have any jobs or internships in college?

Joe: I had a part time job at a machine shop. I highly recommend this to anyone interested in making or designing anything that is metal, plastic, or wood. This experience taught me how things are made. Understanding how things work or are put together is very important. You don't want to come up with a design, and then when you go to make it, you find out it is either very expensive or impossible to manufacture. 3D printing can produce almost anything you can think of, but when it is printed you may find out that the design is not strong enough to withstand use, or it is too expensive, or it takes too long to 3D print.

I had two internships in college. One was with Rexroth, which is now owned by Bosch. They are a hydraulics company. I was responsible for converting old printed blueprints into electronic drawings. The other was working as a mentor for middle school aged students who had special needs or limited abilities. The focus of the program was to modify science experiment kits so that the students with special needs could actually perform experiments and learn science. It was rewarding for me personally. It gave me the opportunity to reach out and have an impact on other people's lives.

CB: What do you do on a daily basis?

Joe: My job is actually very fun and interesting. About fifty percent of what I do I consider pure engineering. It usually starts with a problem that is presented. I might have an opportunity to brainstorm with a team of people from almost every department to try to come up with a solution to the problem. Generally, these ideas we brainstorm are not one hundred percent complete ideas, just the start of an idea or two. All ideas are weighted for their feasibility, practicality, complexity, and ability to be used to solve the problem. The ideas that carry the most weight will be investigated further. For me, "being investigated" means to go off, create a design, build a prototype, and then test it to see if the prototype solves the problem. The majority of the first fifty percent of my day is in the building and testing of prototypes. The other half of my job is regulatory paperwork or other documentation. It is critical to document the development of an idea from inception to tested prototype. The medical device industry is regulated by several agencies both inside and outside the United States. This is necessary when you are making products that have such a significant and potentially life threatening or life saving impact on peoples' lives. As a result, there is a lot of documentation and paperwork that is required.

CB: What are things students should know before pursuing a degree in robotics? Do you recommend it? What skills are important to be good in the field?

Joe: Robotics is a very broad term that can have a lot of meanings. Training or being educated in robotics can prepare you for building autonomous robots for research or automation equipment used in manufacturing. Anything from microchips to automobiles, or it could even mean building robotic hands, arms, or legs for someone who needs assistance. I would recommend a general understanding before deciding what realm of robotics you would like to pursue. Most robots have a body and a brain of some sort. So, a basic understanding would include the basics of programming and mechanical movement.

Another important skill to have is an ability to communicate. You could be the best at what you do in robotics, or in any field, but if you can't communicate well with others, no one will want to work with you. And these days, companies are expecting a lot from teams of people, not just individual contributors. One aspect of communication that sometimes is overlooked is the ability to explain concepts with images. That's a fancy way to say that drawing and sketching are important.

Documentation is also very important. You should get in the habit of writing things down. If you go off and build ten different prototypes, and one works better than the others, how will you remember exactly how that particular prototype was made if you don't have notes to reference?

Finally, the most important skill, in my opinion, to learn for this or any aspect of your life is persistence. If something doesn't work, try again in a slightly different way. You have to understand that nothing will work perfectly the first time you try it. Probably not the second, third, forth, or even hundredth time either. The best engineers that I know are not afraid to make "failures"—dozens, hundreds, and even thousands of "failures" before coming up with something that works. I can honestly say that some of the most interesting, elegant, or complex designs I have developed were done so at the cost of dozens of iterations. That means dozens of failures. Even if something doesn't work the way you want it to, you should learn something from it, and then be persistent in your effort to find what will work the way you want.

CB: What's your favorite thing about your work?

Joe: My favorite thing is building prototypes. For me, the creation of devices or prototypes just to see "what would happen if..." is very fulfilling. Every time I build something new or different, I learn something. Sometimes the lesson is simply "yep, that doesn't work". But if you go one step further and try to add to the statement "that doesn't work because..." that makes you better at your job. Especially, if you have to do some deep investigation as to why something didn't work.

CB: If you could do it over again, would you change anything?

Joe: If I could go back in time and tell my younger self some important things about living, among other things, I would tell myself never stop learning. It is easy to study for a test and to do well, but that information might not truly have sunk in. You must find ways to incorporate things you learn into your life. Otherwise, you will have to go back and re-learn it again when you do need that information. I have spent a lot of time trying to relearn things that I had already

*studied, or I have had to retry figuring out things that I had
already figured out. This is a big waste of time that delays
me from developing the latest and greatest thing.*

MEDICAL ASSESSMENT ROBOTS

Medical assessment and intervention are needed to permit
medical personnel to triage victims and provide life support
functions, such as transporting and administering fluids and
medication. The inability to provide medical intervention was
a major problem at the Oklahoma City bombing, as medical
professionals could not reach victims buried in the rubble. The
objective of medical robots during a disaster is to provide telepresence for medical personnel during the four to ten hours that
are usually required to extricate a victim.

To date, no robot has made a "live save," but they have
increased the efficiency and coverage of rescue and recovery
operations while reducing the risk to responders. Engineers,
programmers, and technologists are needed in this field to design
and develop robots that can expedite life-saving support. For
example, "Survivor Buddy," which is a robot head that stays with
victims and allows survivors to play music, watch videos, and
engage the outside world while waiting for rescue personnel can
help alleviate stress and open communication for the responders.
Although not a search and rescue robot, it can certainly help
monitor victims and allow for the most critically injured to be
evacuated first.

ASSISTIVE ROBOTS

Assistive technology includes devices, such as powered
wheelchairs, talking computers, hearing aids, electronic talking
devices, and any facilities that are modified, including grab bars
for showers and restrooms. Recreational assistive technology,
such as specially adapted skis and fishing poles are also available.

If rehabilitation engineering interests you, watch the Special Olympics to see the assortment of assistive technological devices that are available. Imagine the feeling of power and accomplishment associated with providing a disabled person a sense of independence with a way to meet everyday life challenges successfully, and eliminating some of the challenges associated with having a disability in today's society.

Assistive robots can be divided into three categories:
1. Manipulations Aids – these devices usually involve a robotic hand or arm and aid in holding something.
2. Mobility Aids – these devices include robotic wheelchairs and specially adapted robotic technology that helps people get from point A to point B.
3. Cognitive aids – this may be a robotic system that helps an Alzheimer patient remember to take their medicine, or a system that automatically measures a drug or hormone system within the body and dispenses what is needed.

The applications for robotics continue to increase as the size of electronics, sensors, actuators, and storage devices decrease. This, corresponding with advances in materials, mobility, and control software allow designers to attempt new ways of using electromechanical or mechatronics technology to further explore and improve the well-being of people with disabilities through rehabilitation engineering, which is a popular specialty within biomedical engineering. According to the Biomedical Engineering Society, "Rehabilitation engineers enhance the capabilities and improve the quality of life for individuals with physical and cognitive impairments." (www.bmes.org)

A rehabilitation engineer may work on site with a person recently confined to a wheelchair or help to redesign the person's workspace. For example, changes might include a desk that can be raised and lowered at the push of a button, wider doorways, and indoor ramps. A rehabilitation engineer may also redesign computer systems to assist people with cognitive or physical disabilities. One rehabilitation engineer designed a Braille keyboard to aid blind people to type; another developed a system that enabled people paralyzed below the waist to drive an automobile.

ERADICATING DISEASE ROBOTS

If you are interested in medicine and in particular, eradicating (i.e., getting rid of) disease on a large scale, a career in robotics has a lot to offer. Eradicating deadly epidemics, a task most humans fear, is perfect for a robot.

The opportunities in this area are vast because at present there are no robots that are prepared and ready to be used to handle a deadly virus such as rabies, smallpox, or Ebola. In the case of smallpox during the twentieth century, the disease killed one-third of those infected. The two out of three that survived often had permanent scars and some were blinded. It is estimated that smallpox killed 300 million people during that time period. (www.livescience.com)

Imagine this type of epidemic happening today. If vaccines were available, such as one for Ebola, robots could dispense injections saving the potential accidental infection of emergency responders. Robots could help locate infected animals and possibly help sick people get to medical centers. Robots would be immensely valuable in such a situation.

The Center for Robot-Assisted Search and Rescue (CRASAR) at Texas A&M University is collaborating with the White House Office of Science and Technology and other groups to determine how to design and use robots during future epidemic situations, which will be a new field that might be referred to as Safety Robotics. Using Ebola as the example, current CRASAR Director Robin Murphy listed some possibilities that may be employed based on current discussions:

"Mortuary robots to transport respectfully the deceased, as Ebola is most virulent at the time of death and immediately following death

- Reduce the number of health professionals within the biosafety labs and field hospitals (e.g., automated materials handling, tele-robotics patient care)
- Detection of contamination (e.g., does this hospital room, ambulance, or house have Ebola)
- Disinfection (e.g., robots that can open the drawers and doors for the commercially available "little Moe" disinfectant robot)
- Telepresence robots for experts to consult or advise on medical issues, train, and supervise worker decontamination to catch accidental self-contamination, and serve as "rolling interpreters" for different languages and dialects
- Physical security for workers (e.g., the food riots in Sierra Leone)
- Waste handling (e.g., where is the biowaste from patients and worker suits going and how is it getting there?)
- Humanitarian relief (e.g., autonomous food trucks, UAVs that can drop off food, water, medicine, but also "regular" medicine for diabetes and other illnesses for people who are healthy, but cut off)
- Reconnaissance (e.g., what's happening in this village? Any signs of illness? Are people fleeing?)"

(Murphy, R. (2014). Robots and Ebola. Retrieved from: crasar. org/2014/10/13/robots-and-ebola/)

To work in the design and development of safety robotics means that you not only have to understand the capabilities of a robot's design, but you must understand a disease and how it spreads. In addition, it is critical to understand the mores and culture where a robot will work. You must know this in order to design a robot to be of the most help. If a robot you design is working in an isolated field hospital, it must work in ways that are culturally appropriate for the area. The perfect robot cannot be of any help if people, out of fear or mistrust, will not allow it to do its job.

Robots in Space

In outer space, the environment has no air, little or no atmosphere, and the temperature fluctuates from very hot when the sun shines to very cold when it doesn't. The principle characteristic of space is its high vacuum or nearly total lack of gas molecules. Other space components that affect life are ionizing radiation and very fine dust. The environment is  hazardous to humans and thus ideal for robots. Almost all space exploration involves the use of robots and robot systems.

Robots have been used to:
- Help make repairs in orbit
- Rescue and service malfunctioning spacecraft
- Take pictures
- Inspect the exterior of any space craft or other robot for damage
- Aid astronauts on spacewalks
- Grab rendezvousing spacecraft
- Collect planetary, asteroid, or star samples of soil, dust, or debris
- Explore the solar system and more

Space exploration and particularly deep-space exploration is not possible without the use of robots and robotic systems. Most robotic systems and robots that are used to explore space need a type of intelligence. Being remotely operated doesn't work well because of the speed-of-light and the time delay associated with space to Earth communications. On the moon, the time delay is only a few seconds, but on Mars, the communications

delay is ten minutes or more. In contrast, to communicate with a robot on Saturn or Titan, there is more than an hour delay.

Dating back to 1957 with the release of Sputnik I, space exploration has been dominated by robotic spacecraft. According to Kazuya Yoshida in the *Springer Handbook of Robotics*, any unmanned spacecraft can be called a robotic spacecraft. Space robots are now designed with more capabilities and can manipulate, assemble, and serve as assistants to astronauts while in orbit. They can be designed to extend an astronaut's reach when exploring remote planets. In order to land astronauts on Mars, NASA will need to have robots and rovers in place that are ready to assist humans when they arrive. Robots will become part of an astronaut's everyday existence while on remote planets and celestial bodies.

There are three types of space robots:

1. Orbital Robots – Orbital robots work in orbit. They are usually robotic arms that bring materials and tools to astronauts or are tele-operated to make repairs on the outside of a spacecraft. Orbital robots have been used to complete tasks on the International Space Station (ISS)

and an humanoid robot is used to clean the inside of the orbiting station. Canadarm II, the station's primary robotic arm, and Dextre, (pronounced Dexter) a two-armed robot, work outside and are used to move supplies, equipment, and even astronauts. Canadarm II and Dextre often work together to complete tasks. The fifty-six foot long Canadarm II was initially used to assemble the space station while in orbit and is now used to grab cargo ships that bring supplies to the ISS. Once Canadarm II docks a cargo ship, Dextre, which stands twelve-feet tall and has a thirty-foot wingspan, is used to reach into cargo ships and unload supplies and spare parts. Dextre can handle objects as large as a computer desk or as small as a textbook. Its dexterity is such that it has even been used to fix the camera on Canadarm II.

It's interesting to note that Dextre, at 3400 pounds, was never fully assembled and tested on Earth because it needed the weightlessness of space to avoid being crushed under its own weight. Canadian engineers spent ten years developing the robot, but couldn't test it as a complete unit until it was assembled and ready for service 220 miles above the Earth, orbiting at 15,700 mph! In addition, the systems used to test Dextre had to work at 250 degrees Fahrenheit in the sun and negative 200 degrees in the shade. It's an example of a colossal feat of engineering.

2. Surface Robots – Surface robots or rovers explore the surface of planets, such as Spirit, Opportunity and Curiosity. These robots have been used to move across the surface of Mars. They have taken pictures and collected samples since first deployed in 2003.

3. Lander Robots – Landers are immobile robots that once they are in position will stay that way indefinitely. For example, the Mars Lander was a robot with a seven and one-half foot robotic arm that was stationary on the surface of the red planet. It was used to scrape up ice

and scoop up soil for analysis until it froze to death in the negative 200-degree Martian night.

If you think you'd enjoy working as an astronaut, going on spacewalks, and building rockets and robots, the good news is that you can acquire an engineering degree with any type of specialty. NASA employs nine engineers for every scientist, which gives you many options. They hire:

- Biomedical engineers to make space suits that maintain the body's temperature, protect it from the vacuum of space, and protect it from radiation and micro-meteoroids
- Chemical engineers to help with life support systems.
- Mechanical engineers to design machines and a variety of moving parts.
- Electrical engineers to work on control systems
- Technologists and technicians to build, install, and maintain systems.
- Computer programmers and software engineers to give robots autonomy.

The list goes on.

There are endless opportunities for students in this field and you don't have to narrow your interests to succeed. According to Reliable Robots on the Futures Channel, some engineers might spend their days "...fine tuning a set of million dollar micro-cameras so the rovers can 'see' better while exploring miles of Martian terrain." Or, they might be "...designing tele-operated mini-rovers in an office that looks more like a high tech R&D lab at a toy company than a NASA research facility."

NASA is hiring all types of engineers, technologists, technicians, and programmers to work on robots to improve and refine the systems of:

1. Manipulation–Manipulator systems are used on the ISS and were used on the Space shuttle to help with tasks, such as maintaining the ISS, aiding astronauts on spacewalks,

and docking cargo ships. Designing arms and grippers that work in microgravity applications complicates the issue. A manipulator system requires intelligence in order to properly handle very light or heavy materials.

2. Mobility–NASA's Spirit rover being stuck and stranded in soft sand is an example of the need for better mobility in space robots. The terrain on planets can alternate from rocky to desert and present extreme challenges. Research is currently underway for snake and insect robots to be launched from a surface robot when it reaches an area that is impassable. The snake and insect robots can be tethered or untethered and capable of surveillance that will allow the surface robot to determine how to maneuver the impassable obstacle. A robot within a robot is one option for dealing with hazardous terrain.

3. Tele-operation and autonomy–If robots can explore the solar system while keeping humans out of harm's way, they will require intelligence and the ability to make decisions. To have a robot know that something is interesting, to go to that something, take a sample, and then deposit it in one of several analysis tools onboard is the future of robot autonomy. Robots are needed that will distinguish colors, shapes, textures, and obstacles. Once robots (or maybe swarms of robots) venture out to other planets, they will need sensors and communication capabilities to operate on their own.

4. Extreme environments–In outer space, temperatures can fluctuate between 250 degrees Fahrenheit in the sun to negative 200 degrees in the shade. There is high vacuum, no pressure, ionizing radiation, very fine dust, dust devils, dust clouds, and space junk flying about that require the robots to be designed for these extreme environments and made out of durable materials.

Space exploration is an exciting frontier that will require droves of pioneering and talented engineers, designers,

technologists, programmers, and technicians. The opportunities
are plentiful.

Disaster and Rescue Robots

Mobile disaster robots are robots that are deployed during
natural disasters, such as hurricanes, explosions, floods,
fires, avalanches, volcanoes, mudslides, tsunamis, wildfires,
earthquakes, winter storms, and other accidents. Disaster robots
are especially useful for acts of terrorism, such as mining disasters,
building, bridge or tunnel collapse, chemical emergencies, dam
or levee failures, and train wrecks. These robots are designed to
work as ground, aerial, or marine vehicles. Typical rescue robots
are small and easily portable. The type of robot used in a specific
situation is largely determined by the needs as it relates to the
disaster or rescue mission.

Disaster robots help prevent, prepare for, respond to,
and recover from, as well as assess the increasing number of
complex urban
disasters and
extreme events.
If a disaster has
occurred, it may
be physically
impossible, too
dangerous, or
too inefficient
for a human
responder to

enter the hot zone. Robots do not replace people or dogs, but
rather complement human and canine abilities and reduce
the risk associated with the initial entrance into a dangerous
environment. The results of disasters affect the quality-of-life, the

economy, and the environment. If disasters cannot be prevented, rapid response means there will be less loss of life and result in less long-term injuries with faster economic and environmental recovery. The use of disaster and rescue robots help to make the lessening of the impacts of a disaster possible.

Certain disaster environments present extreme terrains and operating conditions that affect the size, sensor performance, and general robot capability for survivability. A robot designed for disaster and rescue may need to function in openings as small as three centimeters or move horizontally and vertically through debris that may be uneven and hazardous. The robots' design must take into account if it will be exposed to large amounts of groundwater. Marine robots may have to function in currents, avoid debris, complications from tides, and see through dingy waters. They may need to be able to navigate through dirty, muddy environments that can foul cameras and sensors and interfere with moving and using the end-effectors. Robots used in disaster environments may have to operate in extreme heat or explosive atmospheres. They may have to overcome unpredictable winds near buildings, houses, and other structures or may need to function within smoky environments or have protection if they will be exposed to radiation.

If you are interested in the designing of or working with robots in disastrous situations, there are plenty of opportunities. Recent weather patterns suggest that the incidence of catastrophic hurricanes, earthquakes, and other meteorological and geological events is on the rise. Within the field of disaster robotics, you can tailor your interests to specific applications. If you are interested in hiking, backpacking, and skiing, you can develop robots for wilderness search and rescue. If you are interested in working with water, you can develop drones that assess floods and find survivors. If you are interested in national security, you can work with bomb sniffing robots or search and rescue robots that go to work after an explosion.

Most rescue robots are tethered. The reason is that they typically function in satellite, GPS, and wireless-denied environments. When buildings topple, such as the World Trade Center, the density of the fallen materials interferes with GPS and wireless networks. On the exteriors of buildings and bridges, building

Robot investigates the rubble

materials can create shadows that interfere with navigation sensors. Wireless communications can be boosted with more power, but that leads to a trade-off between making the robot larger to carry the power and it becoming too large to be used in the damaged environment. Rescue robots also present challenges for operators and for victims. Robot operators usually have to monitor remotely the rescue robot a long distance from the area the robot is attempting to navigate. The operators have to try to see and understand the world through the robot's camera. The hole into the interior of a building collapse may be too small for humans or dogs to maneuver or not be able to support life due to extreme heat, radiation, or fire. In these situations, a tiny aerial robot is sent in to survey the scene and search for survivors. As a result, its camera will only offer a tiny view into the situation. This can lead to poor performance or errors unless the operators receive proper training.

Rescue robots are used to:
1. Search for people in the interior of structures, such as fallen buildings, tunnels, the wilderness and the ocean. The goal is to search faster and more thoroughly without increasing the risk to survivors or rescuers. The robots

should find potential hazards and help get people out.

2. Provide an overview of the situation by mapping and providing intelligence of the impacted area.
3. Remove rubble to reach survivors or for rebuilding.
4. Perform structural inspection from inside a collapsed structure or on the outside to determine if a building, bridge, or tunnel is in immediate need of repair.
5. Medically assess and triage victims. Rescue robots can provide life support by transporting and giving fluids and medicine.
6. Evacuate people in the hot zone or disaster area and get them to a safe holding place. In chemical, biological, or radiological and nuclear events, the number of victims may be too high for human rescuers to remove—especially in their cumbersome and bulky HAZMAT suits. Robots designed for telemedicine support could also be a huge bonus in this situation.
7. Act as a router, repeater, or booster to extend and enhance wireless communication.
8. Transport equipment and supplies from storage areas to responders in the field or hot zone.
9. Estimate debris volume and cleanup so residents can reenter affected areas and go back home.

Ground, air, or marine rescue robots have been used for thirty-four known disasters or extreme incidents starting with the World Trade Center in 2001 to the 2012 Finale Emilia earthquake. Ground robots have increased the efficiency and coverage of rescue and recovery operations while reducing the risk to responders. The majority of deployments have been to mine disasters or to collapses in urban structures from terrorism, accidents, meteorological, or geological events. After the earthquake and tsunami in Japan in 2011, robots were able to enter and assist in the shut down and cleanup of the compromised Fukushima Daiichi Nuclear Plant, preventing an even larger disaster and loss of life. As of April 2013, there is no record that robots have directly assisted with saving a life. Robots are credited with decreasing the time used to search for survivors, reducing risk to responders, and accelerating economic recovery. Robots are still uncommon in the use of disaster and rescue, and most agencies or stakeholders do not own a recuse robot, increasing the time it takes to get a robot into a hot zone. Rescue robots are generally thought of for the immediate life-saving response for meteorological, geological, human-made, and mining or mineral disasters. But, these robots can be used for recovery operations as well as prevention and preparation.

If designing and working with robots during disasters seems interesting, pick up a copy of the best book written on the subject, *Disaster Robotics* by Robin R. Murphy. Written by a pioneering researcher in the field, Ms. Murphy has participated in fifteen deployments of robots in disaster response and recovery. The book provides insight into the thirty-four documented deployments of robots to disasters that include the 2001 collapse of the World Trade Center, Hurricane Katrina, the 2010 Haiti earthquake, the Deepwater Horizon oil spill, the 2011 Japanese earthquake and tsunami, and numerous mining accidents. Disaster robots that work on the ground, in the air, and in the water are discussed.

Sporting Robots

The sports industry provides entertainment, physical fitness, and health awareness for millions of people around the world. This field is wide open and growing so rapidly that opportunities for robotic applications are plentiful and imaginative. Sports engineering is an excellent means to impact athletes, sports, and businesses. These engineers are some of the most dynamic, innovative, and creative engineers on the planet. Not only is this industry full of diversity, fun, and intriguing opportunities, most of the engineers working with sporting robots became engineers because of their love of sports and they wanted to either increase athletic performance or enhance the sport overall.

Sports engineering is the bridge between classical engineering and sports science. Sports engineers use robots to analyze equipment, sport materials, and the mechanics of sports, as well as athletes and their movement. The engineers strive to design robots that will prevent injuries and increase the achievement of athletes.

Sports Robots as Training Aids

Robots are commonly used as training aids to increase athletic performance. There are:

- Table Tennis Robots–These robots are designed to improve performance of table tennis players. The most common type of table tennis robot is stationary. It is placed at one end of a table tennis table. Using a ball feeder that can be loaded with fifty or more  balls, the robot serves a ball across the table with a predetermined spin, frequency, and oscillation. The robot can also shoot balls with topspin, backspin, left sidespin, right sidespin, combination spin, and even aid players to develop techniques to combat push, chop, serve, counter, lob, or fast loop shots.

- Baseball and Softball Robots–These robots are designed to help with practice and to improve performance of baseball and softball players. A robot can be set to throw overhand fastballs, overhand curves, split- finger fastballs, fly balls, pop-ups, and grounders at a speed chosen by a coach or player. Besides improving player performance, robots are also designed by engineers to help other engineers design baseball bats. Swing robots are used to test bats for impact, speed, and finding a bat's sweet spot.

- Tennis Robots–Similar to table tennis, baseball and softball, a robot can be designed and used to improve tennis shots and overall fitness of tennis players.
- Hockey Robots–These robots are designed to enhance the sport of hockey. There are robots used as automatic hockey passers to help a player retrieve a puck or ball and score a goal.

Modeling Robots that Test Equipment

- Golf Robots–The United States Golf Association (USGA) maintains strict golf ball manufacturing standards so that no golfer has an equipment advantage over another. The USGA tests golf balls with a robot called "Iron Byron" which reproduces golf swings. The average professional golfer swings a driver at 109 mph, which produces a launch speed of 235 feet/second at a ten-degree angle. Iron Byron, in addition to simulating a golfer's swing repeatedly, also performs tests that the USGA can determine if a new golf ball meets the standards specified of a minimum size (1.680 inches in diameter), maximum weight (1.62 ounces), maximum distance (296.8 yards), and initial velocity (255 feet/second).
- Bowling Robots–Bowling is one of those sports where every throw is unique. The amount of oil on the lane, the type of oil, the lane material, the temperature, the humidity, and the type of bowling ball can affect the outcome of each throw. Bowling alleys apply mineral oil on the lanes, which are most commonly made of pine or cherry wood or a synthetic laminate. The lanes are conditioned to take continual pounding. The amount

of oil applied on the lanes closer to the pins is different from the amount lubricating the lanes closer to the bowler. Likewise, the amount of oil on the outside of the lane is less than on the inside. No two bowling lanes have the same amount of oil. Some alleys use different grades of oils, and some lane oiling robots disperse the oil differently along the lane. Balls traveling down a lane can reach temperatures of 1,400 degrees Fahrenheit, push the oil around, and create an endless assortment of oil lines and variables for ball designers. The outer surface or coating a designer puts on a ball can give it grip or allow it to slide through the oil. A semi-dry oiling on a lane can create tracks within the lane that, when followed, can almost guarantee strikes for serious bowlers. The core of the ball can allow it to gyrate (i.e., spin on its axis) and hook more or less in a particular direction. The composition of the ball can allow it to go slower or faster.

With all the variables of oil to consider, bowling ball designers use a robot that is designed to throw a bowling ball down the alley in exactly the same way each time. This allows designers to test prototypes or finished balls under different lane conditions. According to Columbia 300, "... after a prototype has been created, it is then ready for on-lane testing. The robot makes this job easier and allows the engineers to ensure that they are comparing apples to apples when they test two bowling balls. This is where the C.A.T.S. (Computer Aided Tracking System) comes into play. Through a series of on-lane sensors, the robot communicates with the C.A.T.S. that tracks the ball speed, location at various points on the lane, and calculates the entry angle of the ball into the pins, all in the blink of an eye. This information is transferred into a database for comparison against other balls in the test group."

- Swimming Robots–To enhance the sport of swimming, engineers design everything from a swimming pool that reduces turbulence generated by a swimmer to the swimsuit that reduces a swimmer's resistance through the water to the high-tech computerized racing systems used at Olympic events. For example, to help swimmers swim faster, scientists and engineers decided to study fish. Engineers at MIT built a robotic fish to study its movements. From the data, Olympic swimmers, using fish-like wetsuits, have broken many world records.

Robots that Play a Sport
- Soccer–Robot soccer is an excellent example of the complexity involved in creating artificial intelligence. The first Robot World Cup Initiative (RoboCup) was held in Japan in 1997 and has been an annual event ever since. Imagine a robot sensing the location of an orange soccer ball, chasing the ball, and outmaneuvering other players to eventually score a goal. The competitions usually feature teams of robots that range in size from those so small they can compete on a Ping-Pong table-sized field to the size of adult humans. A key goal of the RoboCup competition is to create a team of fully autonomous soccer-playing robots that will beat the human world champion soccer team by the year 2050.

The University of Southern California (USC) competed with five soccer-bots that could spin and twirl on individual spherical truck wheels. The USC soccer-bots were created from modified radio-controlled toy trucks. Each robot received a Pentium-powered brain and a digital eye. The Pentium laptop was mounted onto each robot player's back and connected to the eye. Wei-Min Shen, the computer science professor heading the project said, "The complexity of such a task is extraordinary. Just getting the robot to distinguish between a soccer ball and a human leg requires months of programming. Sometimes, the soccer-bots' eyes detect the red hue in flesh and mistake it for the orange in a soccer ball."

- Sumo Wrestling – Sumo Wrestling is a Japanese form of heavyweight wrestling in which a wrestler wins by forcing his opponent outside of a circular ring or by making him touch the ground with any part of his body except the soles of his feet. In the robotics world, a sumo robot has to find its opponent with ultrasonic proximity sensors and try to push it out of the ring. After pushing the start button, no remote controls are used—the robot is autonomous until the round ends.

As a sports engineer, you can work to improve performance for all athletes, increase the fun and recreation of dedicated fans, and improve the image of all engineers. A sporting robot can be one that assists an athlete to enhance his or her performance, tests sports equipment, or that actually plays the sport itself.

Educational Robots

Science, Technology, Engineering, and Mathematics (STEM) trained workers are in demand all over the world. Educational robotics is a term that is used to describe using robots as educational tools and offers educators a unique alternative to inspire and motivate students. Using an interactive robot, students can review for tests; take quizzes; and practice mathematics, vocabulary, spelling, and other subjects that require memorization or repetition. Robots used in this capacity will not replace teachers, but rather supplement instruction.

FORMAL EDUCATION

For over 20 years, robots have been used in the classroom. Building robots is a very exciting and engaging way to apply science, math, engineering and technology ideas and concepts. In

addition, it promotes spatial visualization, problem-solving and analytical thinking skills.

Pitsco's Tetrix Prime Robot Building System was developed with the goal of having a flexible building system so students could experience the Engineering Design Loop; designing, building and testing prototypes. From that point, subsequent design iterations can be made, observing and recording benefits and disadvantages with each design iteration. The quick building and disassembly time of the Tetrix Prime system is ideal for multiple iterations of robot prototypes.

INFORMAL EDUCATION

Two of the most popular types of informal educational robot venues that interact with the public are (1) robots in competitions and (2) robots that allow interactive, hands-on discovery that entertains and educates visitors in museums.

Robotic Competitions

These competitions are exciting and energetic. Each competition team often consists of a team of students from four to twenty-five and a single robot. Every robot has a specific task to accomplish and no two robots look alike. Based on the goals of the competition, each team designs their robot to perform the task assigned in the best means possible. Creativity, team building, and communication skills are valuable assets that can mean the difference between winning and coming in second.

Robotic competitions have become extremely popular and are a great way to gain exposure to engineering and manufacturing. There are hundreds of robotic competitions every year all around the world. Competitions range and include underwater robots, aerial robots, sumo robots, FIRST Robotics, BEST Robotics, and SeaPerch. These competitions are expanding each year. Prizes include cash, scholarships, T-shirts, and more.

These competitions will help you develop an appreciation of, and interest in, STEM, improve communication and teamwork skills, and help you make lifelong friends. Participating in a robotic competition allows you to get a real-world feeling for the design process and problem solving. They can also help you develop an understanding of the business world and entrepreneurship.

Robots in competitions can be different with varying levels of autonomy.

1. Boosting Engineering, Science, and Technology (BEST) competitions are setup to use robots that are designed to be radio controlled only. The robots do not use independent actions or make decisions. The operators use joystick and game controller devices to navigate and control each robot. This kind of contest emphasizes mechatronics and mechanical design.

2. FIRST competition robots are tele-operated and under the control of an operator, but also include sensors for

feedback that allow some robot processing of commands. These robots also include some autonomous features. This kind of contest emphasizes software and programming in addition to mechatronics and mechanical design.

3. Fully autonomous contests, such as robot soccer or football and sumo wrestling robots do not interact with their robot operators. They can replay a canned set of tasks, use sensors for feedback to adjust their actions, or use those sensors and feedback to learn as they go, such as a person who touches a hot stove, receives a burn, and thereby learns not to touch a hot stove.

Some contests emphasize performance and some focus on opposition. A contest that emphasizes performance ranks a robot against a course. If a robot has to find an item in a maze, and perform required tasks along the way, the team will score well. In an opposition contest, a robot must outperform the other robots. In this case, the robot must find an item in a maze before the other robots can do the same.

For a list of robotic competitions, see the Appendix.

Museums and Science Centers

Educational robots are unlike space robots or military robots that take instructions from a specialist and perform a certain task. Educational robots interact with the general population. They are programmed to perform in specific situations, such as guiding visitors around museums, college campuses, research facilities, laboratories, manufacturing facilities, and other venues that provide tours and educational information. They provide entertainment, therapy with assistive technology, and inspire learning.

Museums and science centers are becoming privately funded multimedia edutainment attractions. Public funding for these institutions is being cut each year. Many analysts think that as more people in the United States begin to retire, the funds available for social programs will begin to dwindle and current funding for the arts and sciences will be cut further. As public funding for museums and science centers has shrunk, private corporations and donors have stepped in to fill the gap. The private sector's keener focus on the bottom line has resulted in a shift toward edutainment.

Robot giving a company tour

The idea for guided museum tours started with robots giving research lab tours. The robots originally were designed with only a vision sensor. Visitors would wave their foot to show the robot that they wanted a tour. The robot was not designed to interact with people and had a preprogrammed route. Later, freely navigating robots were developed to maneuver around in complex buildings, such as large museums and science centers. These newly designed robots had buttons for user input and speech for output. Today, fleets of robots with personality and facial expressions give tours to hundreds of thousands of museum visitors.

There is tremendous opportunity for robotic engineers if this educational trend continues. It will open doors to new venues and avenues for employment. The challenge is to package high-quality entertainment under the guise of an enthusiastic, inspirational, and promotional form of education. This is not an easy task. The trick is to know that being immersed in STEM subjects is not the same as understanding STEM subjects. Creative roboticists will need to create learning environments and opportunities that allow students to interact and play in a way that is inviting, relevant, and entertaining.

Part Four—The Many Approaches to Careers in Robotics

The list below provides the most common majors for future roboticists to work in the robotics industry. The descriptions given are not solely for careers in robotics, but are designed to give an overview of each degree.

Very few colleges specifically teach robotic engineering. You will most likely need to complete a degree in a field that aligns with your interest with an emphasis in robotics, biomedical, computer, electrical, manufacturing, mechanical, or electromechanical applications. The careers and opportunities in this field are endless, as robots become more integrated into society. The careers and degree options are changing as the knowledge of and research in robotics continue. Many up and coming engineers will not only create new robots but new robotic sectors as well.

Common Majors for Robotic Engineering

ROBOTIC ENGINEERING
Average Starting Salary: $ 49,100
Average Salary: $ 94,310

Robotic engineers design and maintain robots and robot systems, and research new applications for robots. Equipped with the proper sensors, robots can inspect the quality of meat, measure the pollution emissions of manufacturing plants, assist in surgery, detect corrosion in sewer pipes, investigate the depths of a volcano, or assess the speed of a tornado. Robots can improve the standard of living and provide more information about Earth or even the solar system. Opportunities of study and advances in the use of robots will open new doors for space or sea exploration.

Robots have been used primarily in the manufacturing industry, which continues to be the primary employer of robotics engineers. Automobiles are often built with the aid of a programmable machine that incorporates great precision, speed, and power. Robotics is also expanding to space exploration, interactive entertainment, healthcare, construction, mining, agriculture, and other fields that are exhausting and repetitive for human workers or are hazardous, dangerous, or undesirable. According to the U.S. Department of Labor, the field is expected to grow thirteen percent by 2018 and become more important in society and the global market. Robotic engineers work closely with computer programmers, electrical, mechanical and manufacturing engineers, and production managers.

In an assembly line process, the manufacturing engineer will evaluate the workflow and decide if a robot is needed and what the robot should do. These specs are given to a robotics engineer who designs the robot along with the control systems, end effectors, actuators, and other required components, and then creates the specs for the various parts within the robot to function properly.

For example, robotic engineers decide how the controls of a robot will work. A mechanical engineer will design a sensor to detect light, food, tilting, and so forth. While the robotics engineer 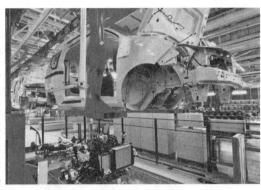 will design how the sensor will be controlled and incorporated into the robot. The robotic engineer will also work with computer programmers, computer engineers, and software engineers to ensure the supporting computer system and software is compatible with the hardware designed by the mechanical engineer and the electronics designed by the electrical engineer.

The most common daily activities performed by robotic engineers include:
- Designing, building, configuring, and maintaining robots and robotic systems
- Increasing the precision of a robot in action, such as when used on an assembly line or in another form of industry
- Refining the control systems, actuators, sensors, or other systems in a robot
- Automating robotic systems to improve efficiency and reliability
- Evaluating robot prototypes and designs
- Researching new applications for robots
- Supporting and maintaining previously installed robots

In the United States, a bachelor's degree in robotic engineering is only taught at Worcester Polytechnic University. Individuals working as robotic engineers most often have degrees in mechatronics, electromechanical engineering, electromechanical engineering technology, electrical, biomedical, mechanical, computer, software, systems and industrial and manufacturing engineering or engineering technology with an emphasis in robotics, systems that robots use or a robotic application (electronics, manufacturing, agriculture, energy, aerospace, etc.)

BIOMEDICAL ENGINEERING
Median Starting Salary: $41,800
Median Income: $81,540

Biomedical engineering is, in a very real sense, people engineering. The objective of biomedical engineering is to enhance health care by solving complex medical problems using engineering principles. Those who specialize in this field want to serve the public, work with health care professionals, and interact with living systems. This broad field allows a large choice of sub-specialties. Many students say they choose biomedical engineering because it is people-oriented.

Biomedical engineers who work in robotics are making lives easier through the:
- Design of tiny robots that can go inside a human body to destroy blood clots.
- Development of Exosuits to help soldiers carry heavy loads.
- Design of tele-robots that can assist doctors in surgery by providing extra light and removing hand tremors in surgeons.

- Development of robots that can take water and medicine to victims trapped in rubble after a natural or human-made disaster.
- Assistance to eradicate diseases, such as Ebola in hospitals.

There is so much more! The opportunities are limited to your imagination.

The biomedical engineering field changes rapidly. New technology is designed and fabricated every day. Biomedical engineers can expect a satisfying career with tremendous diversity and growth potential. The field includes many branches: biomechanical, bioelectrical, biochemical, rehabilitation, clinical, and genetic engineering.  There are also many sub-specialties within biomedical engineering, such as surgical lasers, telemedicine, nuclear medicine, and clinical computer systems.

Examples of specializations within biomedical engineering include:
- Artificial organs, such as hearing aids, kidneys, hearts, blood oxygenators, synthetic blood vessels, pacemakers and joints
- Prosthetic devices, such as arms, legs, hands, feet, fingers, toes, and facial organs

- Automated patient monitoring devices for surgery or intensive care, which include monitoring healthy persons in unusual environments, such as astronauts in space or deep-sea divers
- Blood chemistry sensors for detecting higher or lower levels of potassium, sodium, O_2, CO_2, and pH balance
- Advanced therapeutic and surgical devices, such as laser systems for eye surgery, endoscopic surgery, and automated delivery of insulin
- Computer-based systems for diagnosing diseases and hospital management
- Clinical laboratory design, such as computer analyzers for blood or urine samples and cardiac catheterization laboratories
- Medical imaging, such as ultrasound, computer assisted tomography (CAT), magnetic resonance imaging (MRI), and positron emission tomography (PET) systems
- Physiologic system computer modeling, such as blood pressure control, renal function, seeing and hearing nervous circuits
- Biomaterials design, such as the mechanical, transport, and biocompatibility properties of implantable artificial organs, limbs, and materials
- Biomechanical applications using gait analysis and growth factor applications
- Sports medicine in rehabilitation and physical therapy as well as external support devices

A roboticist with a degree in biomedical engineering has many ways to make a large impact on society. Robots are needed in hospitals, government regulatory agencies, corporations, medical device companies, research labs, and universities. The field of biomedical engineering is very large and almost every aspect of it can benefit from the design and development of robotics.

COMPUTER ENGINEERING

Median Starting Salary: $67,800
Median Income: $98,810

Computer engineering is fast growing, interesting, and very similar to electrical engineering, except that computer engineers work exclusively with computers and computer systems or equipment. Because every robot has a brain or some sort of intelligence, computer engineers, computer engineering technologists, computer scientists, and information technologists are in high demand.

Computer engineers can work in hardware or software, but for the purposes of this guide, computer engineers are those that work on the hardware side and develop hardware technologies, such as robotic architecture, communications, and systems. Software engineers work on the software side. They deal with applications, such as artificial intelligence, and operating systems that run robots, computers, and related systems.

In general, computer engineering deals with the many aspects of computer systems and is full of exciting and diverse opportunities. These engineers may research, design, develop, test, manufacture, or install computer systems, networks, circuit boards, integrated circuits (computer chips), operating systems, software or peripheral equipment, such as keyboards, mice, printers, speakers, or microphones. They may also plan computer layouts or research future applications or environments for computers. For example, computer engineers are responsible for the design of computers that are in robots, automobiles, microwaves, iPods, watches, cell phones, mobile devices, video games, and more. Some computer engineers may be at work right now trying to figure out how to embed computers into shoes that will provide more spring if you are walking or running quickly, prescription eye glasses that can eliminate bi- or trifocals by detecting eye strain, or ovens that can double as freezers and be programmed to turn on, defrost, and then cook your dinner.

Many computer engineers work for large corporations, helping employees with hardware or software problems. They may create, maintain, or install local-area networks (LANs), parallel architecture, multiprocessor architecture, real-time systems, or multimedia within companies. Computer engineers often work as part of a team that designs new robotic hardware, software, and systems. A core team may be composed of engineering, marketing, manufacturing, and design people who work together until the product is released. Computer engineers may also work in research and development to get talking computers, voice-activated automobiles or appliances, and other inventions affordable and to market.

According to the Institute of Electrical and Electronic Engineering (IEEE) computer society, "Computing professionals might find themselves in a variety of environments in academia, research, industry, government, and private and business organizations—analyzing problems for solutions, formulating and testing, using advanced communications or multi-media equipment, or working in teams for product development." Here's a short list of research and vocational areas in computing:

- Artificial Intelligence—Develop computers that simulate human learning and reasoning ability
- Computer Design and Engineering—Design new computer circuits, microchips, and other electronic components
- Computer Architecture—Design new computer instruction sets and combine electronic or optical components to provide powerful, but cost-effective computing

- Information Technology—Develop and manage information systems that support a business or organization
- Software Engineering—Develop methods for the production of software systems on time, within budget, and with few or no defects
- Computer Theory—Investigate the fundamental theories of how computers solve problems and apply the results to other areas of computer science
- Operating Systems and Networks—Develop the basic software computers use to supervise themselves or to communicate with other computers
- Software Applications—Apply computing and technology to solving problems outside the computer field in education or medicine, for example.

ELECTRICAL AND ELECTRONIC ENGINEERING
Median Starting Salary: $57,300
Median Income: $84,540

Electronics are critical to robots. Without some source of power and internal circuitry, a robot does not function. Electrical and electronic engineers (EEs) are imaginative problem solvers who make sure the electronics inside of every robot function as intended. The diverse and progressive field of electrical and electronic engineering has grown rapidly and is one of the largest branches of engineering.

According to the IEEE, "Electrical engineering is about 100 years old, and electronics has been a science for about 75 years. Electrical engineers specializing in power work with motors and generators, and design transmission lines and power plants. EEs specializing in electronics deal with communications, such as radio, television, and cell phones, and with digital and analog circuit technologies. All engineers draw from the fundamentals of science and mathematics. They design and work with electrical, electronic, electro-optical, and electromechanical devices, circuits, and systems. They collaborate with other professionals in developing sophisticated software tools that support  design, verification, and testing. Electrical engineering is a discipline that integrates many other disciplines, such as physics, chemistry, mathematics, computer software and hardware, solid-state electronics, communications, electromagnetics and optics, signals and signal processing, systems science, reliability, engineering economics, and manufacturing."

The developments of electrical and electronic engineers are everywhere. There are thousands of electrical devices and systems available today that electrical engineers have somehow touched. Anything you plug into the wall – stereos, computers, microwaves, televisions, power tools, air-conditioners, and major appliances – has been touched by an electrical engineer. Even things you can't plug into the wall – satellites, cell phone towers, underwater power transmission lines, wind turbine storage devices – have been designed, manufactured, or modified by electrical engineers.

Major specializations within electrical engineering include power plant/energy, communications, optical engineering, and computer engineering. Electrical engineers who specialize in power applications may work for utility companies designing power distribution systems. Or they may work on generating electricity by using alternative energy sources.

Engineers in this area may also decide they want to be a part of the "green economy" and get a job working in renewable energy. In this capacity they may develop the technology to generate, store, or distribute the renewable solar energy harvested from solar panels. They may be responsible for grid connections, designing the transmission lines or the logistics of transporting energy across the land. Or, they may design electrical, computer and automation systems, alarms, and communication systems.

According to the IEEE, "the key to employability is acquiring the knowledge and skill sets in demand by employers. Those who fail to gain or maintain knowledge and skill with tools, such as computer-aided design (CAD) and other software relevant to their work, are disadvantaged. The lack of communication and interpersonal skills, needed to work effectively on teams, can also be a stumbling block."

INDUSTRIAL AND MANUFACTURING ENGINEERING
Median Starting Salary: $58,581
Median Income: $78,160

Industrial and manufacturing engineers design and organize the optimal manufacturing operations and processes that will make the parts necessary for an object to function. You find industrial and manufacturing engineers in automobile production facilities, overseeing plants of the major computer companies, directing six-person mold and die shops that make advanced prototypes, and working on teams in the football-field-sized structures where Boeing assembles jumbo jets. Wherever there's a production process to be designed and managed, you'll find industrial and manufacturing engineers at work.

In an assembly line process, an industrial engineer is the person who may say that an industrial robot is needed to assemble a particular part. They may inspect the robots and recommend different end effectors or manipulators to perform a job more efficiently. The industrial engineer takes a broad look at the manufacturing process and determines if it can be improved, thereby making the environment safer for employees and saving employers time and money. A manufacturing engineer will go to work once the robot is in place, and will focus on getting the robot to perform it function in the most efficient and effective way possible. This is referred to as process optimization and is the overarching goal of all manufacturing engineers.

Manufacturing engineers need an aptitude for basic engineering principles, a disciplined approach to work, and creativity. Because the focus is the process, not the individual part, the manufacturing engineer needs to look through a wider-angle lens. They bring their particular brand of insight to the teams they work with, such as plant managers, production supervisors, CNC programmers, quality managers, product designers, and R&D staff. The issues the team addresses may range from evaluating new technology and choosing equipment and suppliers to leading industry-wide standards development or reorganizing a plant into a more efficient production system.

Negotiation skills and the ability to sell ideas are essential for the manufacturing engineer. Ford Motor Co. names interpersonal skills right after basic engineering on the list of skills manufacturing engineers need. Ford's manufacturing engineers must work closely with product designers and communicate with them at the same technical level. The goal is not to make a designer out of the manufacturing engineer, but to get design and manufacturing to work seamlessly together in order to make products of the highest quality and at the lowest possible cost.

During the last two decades, most major U.S. companies have turned their attention to the plant floor, discovering that the way they make their products can be a strategic advantage in the growing global marketplace. Manufacturing engineers led the way by championing key concepts including lean production, agile manufacturing, re-engineering, and continuous improvement.

Industrial and manufacturing engineers must do more than make and deliver products competitively. They must use system thinking to understand what role manufacturing plays in the overall business and how to customize products to meet the needs and suit the tastes of customers around the world.

MECHANICAL ENGINEERING
Median Starting Salary: $58,600
Median Income: $78,160

Mechanical engineers are the wheels of the world. In this career, the central topic of concern is the motion of everything: mobile robots, automobile wheels and systems, roller coasters, the inner workings of machines, and the motions of microscopic particles in a nanotechnology research facility or laboratory. This type of engineering is one of the broadest, oldest, and most diverse disciplines. Almost every object you use today was due to the handiwork of a mechanical engineer.

Their creations can directly or indirectly benefit society and make an impact on all of us. Not many people can perform their jobs without their expertise. Mechanical engineers use the principles of energy, mechanics, materials, mathematics, and engineering sciences to research, design, develop, test, and manufacture every kind of vehicle, power system, machine, and technological system (e.g., jet engines, steam engines, power plants, underwater structures, tractors for food production, hydraulic systems, transportation systems, medical devices, energy systems, sports equipment, smart materials, materials and structures for space travel, manufacturing processes, and measurement devices). Any type of machine that produces, transmits, or uses power is most likely the product of a mechanical engineer. Their job involves testing, quality assurance, manufacturing, research, design, development, operations, management,

production, marketing, sales, or product maintenance for large companies, small firms, or for themselves as consultants. There is hardly any aspect of life that has not been influenced by a mechanical engineer.

According to the Department of Labor, by the year 2018, there will be an additional 87,000 jobs for mechanical engineers. Mechanical engineering is listed as one of the top fifty occupations with the most openings that require a bachelor's degree. The job is highly individualistic and flexible because it is so broad. However, engineering is still very team-focused, especially in robotics, which demands many disciplines working together. Because so many companies and government facilities need machines and systems to be more competitive in today's global marketplace, graduates will find a substantially increased ability to make a good salary doing what they want and living where they want.

The trends forecasted for a career in mechanical engineering include:

- The design of robotic systems that can increase mobility, assist first responders in disaster situations, improve healthcare, and enhance space flight.
- The creation of new materials featuring remarkable attributes of strength and lightness.
- The miniaturization of medical instruments and other tools.
- Flexible and programmable manufacturing systems allowing rapid switching from one product to another.
- Energy technologies development, such as fuel cells, solar energy, wind farm development, more fuel efficient or alternative energy transportation systems, and management of environmental waste and hazards in compliance with stringent government regulations.
- Enhancement of the role of personal computers in engineering design and analysis.

An increasing number of mechanical engineers will be needed to design and develop devices for the general public that will help to make their lives more convenient, cost effective, easier, more efficient, and more comfortable. These products maybe anything, such as washers and dryers, cell phones and other electronic gadgets, or airplanes and other forms of transportation.

Essentially, you can combine almost any other technical interest, such as robotics, internal combustion, computers, telecommunications, biomedical engineering, mechanics, materials, nuclear energy, alternative energy, noise control, aerospace, or something not yet invented with a degree in mechanical engineering.

SOFTWARE ENGINEERING

Median Starting Salary: $67,800
Median Income: $98,810

Software engineering is on the cutting edge of technology. As the world becomes more computerized, software engineering, a very progressive field, is in high in demand. Software enables us to use robots and computers. A software program is the translator between humans and computers. Without software, a computer would be collection of machine parts, unable to do anything, and a robot would not be able to receive instructions.

Software engineers apply the principles and techniques of computer science, engineering, and mathematical analysis to the design, development, testing, evaluation, analysis, and maintenance of the software, apps, operating systems, compilers, and network distributions that enable computers to perform their many applications. In programming, or coding, software engineers instruct a computer, cell phone, or mobile device how to perform a specific function. They must have strong problem solving and programming skills, but may be more concerned with developing algorithms and analyzing and solving programming problems than with actually writing of the code. Computer programmers will usually write the code and work with a software engineer. Anyone in this field must be prepared to be a life-long learner. The field changes quickly as companies' race to market with new ideas and concepts to stay on the cutting edge of computer design and software development.

The current demand for software engineers far exceeds the supply. In the robotics world, software engineers can enjoy a bright and diverse future as more applications for robots become available, manufacturers and the general public wants to do more with less, and robotic systems become more precise and refined. To prepare for a career in software engineering, you need to gain exposure to as many programming languages as possible. Popular job requirements include the computer languages of C/C++, Objective C, Unix, Pearl, Python, Java, PhP, HTML, CGI Coding, Visual Basic, and Novell.

SYSTEMS ENGINEERING
Median Starting Salary: $58,581
Median Income: $78,160

According to the systems engineering department at George Mason University, "Systems Engineering is the people-oriented engineering profession. Systems Engineers determine the most effective ways for an organization to use all of a given system's components—people, machines, materials, information, and energy."

Systems engineers plan, design, implement, and manage complex systems that assure performance, safety, reliability, maintenance at a reasonable cost, and on-time delivery. Systems engineers take pieces or parts from several different sectors and integrate them into a complete unit or process. For example, a systems engineer working in the telecommunications industry to develop a new disposable cell phone or telephone system may work with computer or software engineers to develop a program, with mechanical engineers to design the parts, and with electronic engineers to design the circuit boards. Most systems have mechanical or electrical aspects and may include one or more computers as well. A systems engineer is a specialist with integrating the pieces of a system into a process or into an effective whole. For example, an automobile is an integrated system. Electrical engineers create the electrical aspects, such as the ignition and the dashboard. Materials engineers work with the materials aspects, such as designing for aerodynamics or developing puncture resistant tires. Mechanical engineers deal with the mechanical aspects, such as creating high performance suspensions or lubrication systems. The systems engineer is responsible for bringing all of these components together to produce the car. For the systems engineer the challenge associated with a complex system is to foresee or handle side effects that may occur when separate parts are brought together. The dashboard or suspension may not meet the aerodynamics specifications of the materials engineer and the tires may not meet the suspension specifications of the mechanical engineer. The individual products may need to be redesigned in order to work together.

Have you ever wondered how supermarkets and large stores keep their inventories of goods in balance? How they deliver those goods on time? How computers and automobiles are manufactured with quality and at competitive prices? How 1-800 and calling-card calls are handled and routed automatically through the telephone network? How thousands of airplanes and millions of travelers are scheduled and managed efficiently on a daily basis? The answer to all of these questions is systems engineering.

Common Majors for Robotic Engineering Technology

BIOMEDICAL ENGINEERING TECHNOLOGY (BMET)
The Average Starting Salary For a Graduate With:
Bachelor's Degree in BMET is $35,000
Associate's Degree in BMET is $30,000

Biomedical engineering technologists and technicians (BMETs) are responsible for medical technology that enhances health care. BMETs are on the front line of health care, providing installation, design, manufacturing, training of hospital staff and personnel, and preventive maintenance for vital medical equipment. New robotic systems, such as tele-surgery computer systems, equipment, and tools and hospital delivery systems (i.e., food for patients and supplies for providers) are all systems that need to be installed and maintained by BMETs. The work of the BMET individual ensures that all health care professionals are able to provide the care and treatment that patients require.

Biomedical engineering technologists and technicians focus primarily on medical equipment for hospitals and medical service providers. These positions require that the BMET person work closely with physicians, nurses, therapists, hospital staff, and other technical professionals to understand, assess, and make certain the diagnostic and therapeutic equipment and life-saving devices are operating within specifications. This field is similar to clinical engineering, and some BMET graduates are called clinical engineers. The difference is that clinical engineers, with a bachelor's degree in biomedical engineering, may be more involved in design, modification, and pre-purchase assessments whereas the BMETs may be more application-oriented and involved in installing, modifying, inspecting, testing, calibrating, or repairing the equipment after installation. In addition, a BMET graduate might be more likely to work in a hospital or clinical setting, while a biomedical engineer would most likely work at a company.

BMETs must be quick thinkers and problem solvers. If any equipment breaks down in the middle of a procedure and a patient's life is held in the balance, the BMET will be called in STAT in order to fix the problem. Problems that arise could be as simple as a circuit breaker tripping in an operating room to a delivery robot malfunctioning on its way to assist a patient.

Currently, there are only a few ABET (Accreditation Board for Engineering and Technology, Inc., is a non-governmental organization that accredits post-secondary education programs in "applied science, computing, engineering, and engineering technology) accredited biomedical engineering technology programs in the United States. However, many schools offer programs in electronic engineering technology with an emphasis in medical instrumentation, robotics, and electromechanical engineering technology.

COMPUTER ENGINEERING TECHNOLOGY(CompET)

The Average Starting Salary For a Graduate With:
Bachelor's Degree in CompET is $35,000 - $45,000
Associate's Degree in CompET is $25,000 - $35,000

Computer engineering technologists and technicians are often considered modern day heroes. They work with hardware or software issues. When computer users can't figure out how to install or maintain their computers or systems, the technician is called to save the day. When companies need custom applications and network systems designed, they call the computer-engineering technologist. In this age of heavy computer usage, with companies using computers for a large variety of functions, the computer engineering technologists and technicians are invaluable in keeping equipment running, updating software, maintaining connectivity, and interfacing with users.

In the robotics industry, computer engineering technologists and technicians typically work for companies of various sizes where they install, test, operate, and maintain robots and robotic systems as well as the company systems. Common work locations include manufacturing facilities (i.e., robotic and otherwise);  industries that use robots, such as automotive, aerospace, agriculture, and healthcare; research facilities; and educational institutions.

Technicians in this field may find themselves traveling to help restore a robot that was malfunctioning, troubleshooting problems, or helping with software applications. If the technician works for a robot manufacturer, they may give technical support over the telephone and build customer systems in a laboratory. The career paths in this field are varied, flexible, and abundant.

The exact job and responsibilities of a technologist vs. a technician depend on the amount of education, the experience required, and the employer. In general, the technologist with a bachelor's degree will have more responsibility and may be in charge of transforming a concept into a prototype or product. They may have to look at design specifications and know what materials are available to bring an idea to reality. A technician with an associate's degree may take a prototype or product developed by the technologist and run tests to confirm the specifications and ensure the design of the prototype or product is working as intended. However, in this field, experience plays a far greater role in defining job description and responsibilities than educational paperwork.

ELECTRONIC / ELECTRICAL ENGINEERING TECHNOLOGY (EET)

The Average Starting Salary For a Graduate With:
Bachelor's Degree in EET is $35,000 - $45,000
Associate's Degree in EET is $25,000 - $35,000

Electronic engineering technologists design, develop, and manufacture everything that you plug into the wall—televisions, computers, refrigerators, microwaves, and stereos. They design, develop, and work on and work with the electronic components that are in every device that requires electricity for power. These engineers study robots; electronic equipment, such as communication equipment; radar, industrial, wireless, and medical monitoring or control devices; navigational equipment; and computers. They also manage and support cars that today have many electronic components, such as GPS, phones, Internet, and electronic devices that allow a car to park without the intervention of a driver and a navigational systems that allow directions to be given verbally to tell a car to go to a specific place, and then the car will drive to that location autonomously. Electronic engineering technologists also apply their skills to the generation and transmission of electricity. Many electrical engineering technologists work in green energy companies that involve the research, design, and development of solar panels, wind turbines, wave energy and geothermal design.

Electronic engineering technicians repair and maintain electronic equipment used by businesses or individuals. They may work in product evaluation and testing, using measuring and diagnostic devices, such as oscilloscopes, computer software and multi-meters to adjust, test, and repair equipment. They may build circuit boards for use in robots and for testing.

Electronics have revolutionized the world. Everything from iPods, cell phones, or GPS systems contains electronic components. Every business from a small shop owner, utility companies, or federal government agencies needs technologists and technicians. The opportunities are far-reaching and abundant. The engineering technologist or technician can help companies run smoother and more efficiently, such as the following:

- The small shop owner and large companies may not have a technician on staff, but when a machine breaks down, they call a field technician to fix the problem. The field technician may be responsible for installing and ensuring the normal operation of machines located within several companies in a certain geographic area. When equipment breaks down, the technician will first check for common causes of trouble, such as loose connections or obviously defective components. If routine checks do not locate the trouble, the technician may refer to schematics or repair manuals that show connections and provide instructions on how to locate problems. If a machine cannot be repaired on-site, the field technician will arrange to transport the machine to a facility or repair shop where a bench technician can repair it. Some equipment may give an alarm if failing and other equipment may just break. The technician will likely be working on equipment from different technological eras.

- Alternative energy companies may hire technologists to design, develop, or manufacture equipment for wind turbines and farms, solar panels and car recharging stations, or equipment to harvest and transmit energy from dams or other sources of electricity.
- Utility companies will hire engineering technologist as plant or electrical system operators. They hire technicians to do everything, such as installing, operating, maintaining, and controlling electric substations, and monitoring equipment and electric transformers that distribute electricity to homes and businesses.
- Federal government agencies hire technologists and technicians to maintain national security equipment, air traffic control systems, U.S. postal facilities, equipment in customs offices, the U.S. Mint, the Federal Reserve, the White House, and NASA space centers.

ELECTROMECHANICAL ENGINEERING TECHNOLOGY

The Average Starting Salary For a Graduate With:

Bachelor's Degree in Electromechanical Engineering Technology is $35,000 - $45,000

Associate's Degree in Electromechanical Engineering Technology is $25,000 - $35,000

Students interested in applied robotics, the fusion of both mechanical engineering technology and electronic engineering technology, will appreciate the electromechanical engineering technology option. When you think of machines that require electricity and have moving parts, such as robots, printers, automobiles, and draw bridges, they all involve electromechanical engineering technology.

Electromechanical engineering technicians combine fundamental principles of mechanical engineering technology with knowledge of electrical and electronic circuits to design, develop, test, and manufacture electrical and computer-controlled mechanical systems. This field exposes students to  microprocessors, industrial controls, manufacturing processes, instrumentation, and factory automation. Students will use computers to solve problems or run simulation test cases, build databases, and use graphics to complement and supplement problem solving skills.

This field is similar to, and a part of, robotic engineering. The difference is that robotic engineers, with a bachelor's degree in robotic, electrical, mechanical, manufacturing, biomedical, or computer or software engineering, may be more involved in design, modification, and pre-purchase assessments of robots whereas the electromechanical engineering technicians is more application-oriented and involved in installing, modifying, inspecting, testing, calibrating, or repairing the robot. In addition, an electromechanical engineering technician might be more likely to work in a manufacturing facility, while a robotic engineer might work at the same manufacturing facility or a robot design company. Currently, there are only seven accredited programs in the United States for electromechanical engineering technology.

MANUFACTURING ENGINEERING TECHNOLOGY
The Average Starting Salary For a Graduate With:
Bachelor's Degree in Manufacturing Engineering Technology is $42,634
Associate's Degree in Manufacturing Engineering Technology is $29,175

Manufacturing engineering technologists and technicians work with engineers to customize existing manufacturing processes related to the manufacturing of products. They plan, test, produce, and fabricate consumer and industrial products and can serve as a communications bridge between the shop floor and management. They may find themselves developing processes for a small office to manufacturing systems in football field sized buildings. Regardless of the size of the business, manufacturing engineering technologists and technicians are tasked with continually improving the manufacturing process in order to improve product quality and per piece profits.

Manufacturing Engineering Technology is an exciting career path focused on the application of technology in high-tech environments, using computer-aided design, CNC operations, robotics, lasers, and microprocessor controls to manufacture the products that society needs and wants. Technologists and technicians may find themselves planning, designing, testing, and analyzing processes and systems, inspecting operations, running tests on particular areas of the system, managing projects, supervising production lines, writing reports, communicating with other members on the team, and giving presentations about their findings.

Technologists are involved in all stages of design and manufacturing and work in a wide variety of firms—a few of these include aerospace and telecommunications companies, sports equipment companies, and consumer product related companies. These graduates may work in manufacturing facilities; federal, state or local government agencies, such as the U.S. Postal Service; medical device companies; computer equipment companies; and many more. Technologists are well prepared to perform in such positions as manufacturing engineer, quality assurance engineer, production engineer, project engineer, and facilities engineer. They may also work in technical sales and technical services, representing manufacturers of production equipment.

Although the schooling to become an engineering technologist is still four years, it is slightly less calculus intensive than

manufacturing engineering. The focus is on hands-on experience and the application of ideas using scientific principles. Graduates will have an excellent understanding of casting, forming,  machining, and fabricating processes that are used by today's leading manufacturing companies. The two extra years of education that separates a technologist from a technician provides significant opportunities for advancement into management of manufacturing engineering, production operations, or technical sales.

- A technologist with an interest in business may estimate labor costs, equipment life, and facility space requirements.
- Depending on the employer, a technologist with an interest in design may work on the processes that create consumer products, such as candy, motorcycles, kitchen equipment, snowboards, music technologies, military ships and aircraft, and wireless devices.

- Technologists may also work in food technology to make sure breakfast cereals or frozen waffles are delivered to the right supermarkets on time, on budget, and are processed efficiently and safely.

Students can also attend two-year colleges and graduate with an associate's degree to become a technician or continue to the bachelor's degree. Technicians work for the same companies and are the hands-on people involved in the installation, maintenance, and repair of the same manufacturing and control systems and processes. They are trouble-shooters who take the engineers' design or concept and turn it into a product with attention to manufacturability, quality assurance, and cost-effective production using engineering principles, computers, and software along with their practical technical skills. It is an exciting field rich in opportunities not only locally or statewide but around the world.

MECHANICAL ENGINEERING TECHNOLOGY
The Average Starting Salary For a Graduate With:
Bachelor's Degree in
Mechanical Engineering Technology is $37,500
Associate's degree in
Mechanical Engineering Technology is $31,250

Mechanical engineering technologists and technicians work with engineers to design, develop, manufacture, and test various kinds of machines, components, and products. Anything with moving parts falls under the domain of mechanical engineering and mechanical engineering technology. Technologists and technicians may find themselves planning, designing, testing, operating and analyzing machines, processes, and installations. They may inspect operations and maintain, install, or operate components or run tests on parts and equipment in a laboratory.

They may also write reports, communicate with other members on the team, and give presentations about their findings.

Mechanical engineering technologists are heavily involved with different aspects of design—solid modeling, finite-element analysis, tolerance stack-up, and mechanism synthesis. They are involved in manufacturing and may work in consulting firms; manufacturing facilities; federal, state, or local government agencies, such as Federal Aviation Administration and the Department of Defense; material testing laboratories; medical device companies; computer equipment companies or service providers; telecommunications companies; utility companies; and many more.

Mechanical engineering technicians may work for the same companies as mechanical engineers and engineering technologists, and may be involved in the installation, maintenance, and repair of machines, manufacturing systems, and control systems. They are the hands-on people—trouble-shooters—that use available materials, engineering principles, and their practical technical skills to take the engineer's design or concept and turns it into a machine, system, or product. It is an exciting field with rich opportunities available around the world. For example,

- A technologist who works in quality control could make sure that products are made to specification.

- A technologist in middle management could serve as the communication bridge between engineering and the manufacturing or production facility.
- In an industrial plant, a technician could remanufacture old equipment in order to recycle or revive its purpose.
- A technician or technologist with an interest in education could become a machine operations trainer, making sure the staff of hospitals or companies and individuals understands the safe and effective procedures for using new equipment.

COMPUTER SCIENCE
Average Starting Salary: $64,100

Computer science deals with automation and what can be efficiently automated. It is the study of computers and the

systems used for computation. Using a combination of science, engineering, and mathematics. A computer scientist delves into the design, development, theory, and applications of software and software systems. This usually includes working with artificial intelligence, multiple programming languages, databases, computer networks, web based systems, vision and

graphics systems, security systems and bioinformatics (e.g., Human Genome Project).

Computers are used to make redundant or tedious tasks more manageable, to solve problems, process data, communicate with each other, and design and analyze user interfaces, algorithms, and security systems. However, knowing how to program is only one aspect of what a computer scientist understands.

According to the Missouri University of Science and Technology, the major areas of Computer Science include:
- Operating Systems—concerned with the development and structure of complex programs that facilitate human-machine communications.
- Computational Science—the analysis of numerical methods for solving mathematical problems with a computer.
- Programming Languages—the study of the design and properties of languages by which humans communicate with computers.

- Architecture—the study and use of mathematical logic to design electronic circuits.
- Intelligent Systems—concerned with the means by which computers may perform tasks that might be characterized as intelligent if performed by humans.
- Automata Theory—an abstract study of computers and their capabilities.
- Information Storage and Retrieval—the study of methods for storing a vast amount of data in a computer and methods for searching and retrieving the stored data.
- Software Engineering—the study of tools and techniques for software design, development, testing, and maintenance.

Part five–Getting Started

Become Well-Rounded

Companies, in an effort to be competitive, want to hire people who can wear many hats, work well in teams, and communicate effectively. When it comes to inspiration, conceptualization, and rock-solid prototypes that work, every engineering discipline is important. The various fields of study need to have individuals who can working well in teams and communicate effectively.

For example, it is necessary to have programmers who understand design and designers who can effectively communicate their work. Engineering and technology students must study multiple disciplines in order to be well rounded and creative in their thinking. In the field of robotics, it is possible to work with other roboticists, engineers, scientists, private entrepreneurs, inventors, investors, technicians, urban planners, accountants, politicians, and policy makers. The collective knowledge of the entire group or team is needed to work through the challenges and problems the team was hired to solve.

It's like playing in a band—the guitarist sets the bass line or melody, the drummer sets the rhythm, and the singer adds words

117

and meaning. Each person doing what he or she does best while working together makes beautiful music. Each player brings different strengths to the band, and the band will not function as efficiently or achieve the sound it wants without each part. Teamwork is integral to the success of a band. Engineering design works in the same way. Each member of an engineering team contributes according to his or her individual strengths, and as a result, society receives new products, benefits from improved manufacturing, and an increased quality of life.

In addition to learning what are the opportunities for working with robots or in the field of robotics, it is necessary to begin to have experiences that will enable you to begin to learn what areas of interest to you. The following are a few examples that will give you such opportunities:

Summer Camps

Summer camps provide another innovative approach to preparing for a career in robotics or evaluating if that career is right for you. Find out what it is like to study robotics. In a summer camp, you will learn about the different types of degrees involved and what they do on a daily basis. Almost every college of engineering offers a summer camp for high-school students. These camps offer a week or two of fun while developing leadership, professional, and personal organizational skills. The camps provide opportunities to meet and talk with engineers during visits to local robotic or engineering companies. Check with the college of engineering at a university near you to see what summer programs are offered, or visit the Engineering Education Service Center's Web site at www.engineeringedu. com to find a camp in your area.

National Robotics Week and Robotics Competitions

The second week of April is National Robotics Week. With events in all fifty states, take the time to find one, and plan to go see what robotics is all about. Events range from demos and tours to competitions. Some of the robotics competitions may include FIRST Robotics, which is a great way to meet other students in engineering and learn what you might like through the sounds, sights, and feel of a competitive event.

You've Decided to Pursue a Robotics Education—What Now?

Now that you have decided to pursue a robotics education, you should prepare for it as soon as possible. Search the Internet for engineering and robotics societies and companies that interest you. Browse their Web pages. Contact them and ask about their programs. This will help you begin to learn more about the field of study as you make your plans for college. Ask to talk to students currently participating in the programs that are offered that interest you.

You can also take advantage of what local engineering firms may have to offer you as you begin to research about the field of robotics. Contact the local firms and ask for a tour. Most firms are happy to show you around and explain what they do. Several companies encourage continuous improvement in engineering education. For example, a company may have a summer intern program that allows college-level science students to work at their facility each year. They may sponsor a job-shadow program to bring junior high and high school students into their facilities or labs to see what researchers are doing. This will give you an immediate opportunity to see the field of robotics in action.

If you like the companies you've contacted, ask if they offer summer internships or job shadowing programs. Through this simple effort, you will make a contact, and more importantly, a potential job opportunity may await you when you finish your degree.

Choosing the Right School

Choosing the school that is right for you is as important as wheels are to automobiles. Your choice should incorporate your preferences. The advantages and disadvantages of each school will depend on your personal needs and wants. Important considerations for most college-bound students include location, cost, faculty, school size, and academics.

1. Location: In addition to distance from home, location refers to the climate and the types of industry in the surrounding area. If there is an industry specific to your degree, then opportunities for summer internships, co-op programs, and part-time work experience increase dramatically. These work experiences often lead to jobs after graduation.

2. Cost: Cost of attendance may be a critical factor in determining the school to select, although your decision should not be based on cost alone. Generally, public institutions are less expensive than private schools, but there are many ways to fund your education at an institution. Most engineering societies offer scholarships, and the government offers grants and loans. Part-time

work, co-op programs, and campus jobs also help reduce the cost of attendance. Check with each financial aid department of the schools you are interested in order to see what grants and loans you may qualify. Call the engineering department to learn about scholarships offered to incoming students through the college. The military may also offer opportunities for financing your education. The National Guard is a popular program among college students. The Air Force, U.S. Coast Guard, Marines, Merchant Marine, Army, and Navy offer education at reduced cost in exchange for a commitment to serve in the Armed Forces for a certain period of time.

3. Faculty: A quality faculty provides for an opportunity to acquire a good education. A faculty that includes women and minorities will broaden your experience and better prepare you to work with people from diverse backgrounds. Faculty members can bring numerous experiences and expertise to their lectures. Check to make sure the faculty rather than graduate students teach the classes you expect to take. As you proceed to your junior-level and senior-level classes, the research of the faculty becomes more important. Try to select a school that has at least one faculty member performing active research in your area of interest. That person can serve as a role model. You are able to talk with and to learn from someone whose interests you share.

4. School Size: School size matters for some students. Large schools offer a greater diversity of people and more things to do, but often lack the professor-student interaction found at smaller schools. In a small school, you may get to know a larger percentage of classmates, but in a larger school you can meet more people. You can receive an excellent education at a large school or a small one; which one you choose is a matter of preference.

5. Academics: Academics is probably the most important factor in choosing the school that is best for you. The

program should be accredited by the Accreditation Board for Engineering and Technology (ABET). ABET accreditation ensures that the program follows national standards for faculty, curricula, students, administration, facilities, and institutional commitment. By choosing an ABET program, you can be sure that the faculty meets certain national standards and that the engineering program is highly regarded by the profession.

Some students like the competitive atmosphere that accompanies attending a very prestigious school, and some students find they work better in a more relaxed environment. Both will require a great deal of studying, although some programs will be more challenging than others. Pick the atmosphere that best fits your personality and aspirations. Questions you might ask yourself at this point are: Do I want to be on the cutting edge of technology? Do I want to find better solutions, even if a current solution already exists to existing identifiable problems? Do I want a combination of the two?

You should find out if free tutoring is offered and if the professors post their office hours. Learn what options are available to help you be successful, such as Can you e-mail questions to professors? Will your questions be answered in a timely fashion? Another consideration is the campus library. Is it easy to find the information you are looking for? Does the school have a special engineering library or carry journals that are specific for your topic of interest, such as robotics?

Student chapters of professional organizations are fun to join. These organizations are an excellent resource during your college experience and in your career search. Many offer opportunities to compete with other colleges in various fields of study. Check to see if the society for the branch of engineering you want to study has a student chapter at the schools you are considering.

Other school selection criteria to consider include sports facilities, leisure activities, community events, cultural events, and campus activities.

The Successful Student

Engineering is a rigorous and demanding major. To be successful in an engineering school, you will need certain life skills. You must be self-disciplined, organized, and manage your time effectively. In college, the real learning often takes place outside the classroom, and less time is spent in the classroom. A general rule of thumb is that for every hour spent in a classroom, engineering students should expect to spend three hours outside the classroom compared with two hours for non-technical majors. A good

time-management system will allow you to participate in extracurricular activities, which broaden your experience and will be of interest to your potential employers.

Engineering curricula vary from school to school; however, most schools do not require you to declare a specific field of interest until the end of your second year. The first two years of engineering school are focused on learning the fundamentals, such as chemistry, calculus, physics, and mechanics (i.e., statics and dynamics). Courses in English, the humanities, and biology are usually also required.

The third and fourth years of engineering school are most often spent studying your chosen specialty. Most universities require their students to complete a design project during their senior year. The project may involve working in teams or individually and involves solving a real-world problem. Students may be able to select a problem of personal interest or a local industry may present a problem that they are currently exploring. Typically, the project requires a research report, the presentation of the design process, and an analysis of the results.

Co-ops and Internships

A cooperative, or co-op, educational experience is one where a student alternates academics with work experience in government, industry, or business. For example, a student may do a parallel co-op where they work part-time and go to school part-time, or complete a traditional co-op where they work for six months and go to school for six months. A good co-op program may be the perfect answer for a non-traditional student who has financial responsibilities.

Amanda Nixon, a mechanical engineering graduate of Kettering University said:

"I interned/co-opted at FANUC America Corporation during the 4 years during my college career. That is, two years' experience total upon graduation since Kettering students intern full time six months out of the year. During this internship, I worked within five different departments in the company. One month after graduating, I started a full time position in the Material Handling Segment at FANUC America Corporation. I provided product and customer support while I was also responsible for aiding in the design, build, and programming of different robot demo cells for various tradeshows throughout the year. This will give me the opportunity to be exposed to many different engineering fields, which I believe to be one of the perks of being in robotics."

(A. Nixon. Personal Communication. February 21, 2015)

Because a co-op program usually takes longer to complete, your experience can be more meaningful. Additionally, a co-op experience will show employers that you have experience and a strong desire to work in your chosen field. In today's competitive market, you need to do everything possible to stand out.

An internship is another method you can use to help you network and become known in your chosen field of study. They generally consist of a summer job at a company that is related to your major. David Tanaka of Industrial Light and Magic began his successful career by interning every summer. By the time he graduated, he was the first choice when a position became available. If you are interested in obtaining an internship position at an engineering firm, find a company you like and apply (i.e., send a resume) as early in the school year as possible.

Summary:
- Take as many mathematics and science classes in high school as possible.
- Get involved in extracurricular activities, such as robotics clubs.
- Practice your communication skills.
- Enter robotics, engineering, or technology competitions. There is a feeling of satisfaction when you see your robot respond and move when you ask it to.
- Tour colleges. See what kinds of projects students on campus are doing, and try to figure out if you would enjoy going to school there. While on campus, talk to engineering, technology, and computer science students about their experiences.
- Take night and summer classes at your local community college. College-level classes are sometimes free for high school students. Take classes that are not offered at your high school with a focus on subjects that might be fun to learn about.
- Visit the web sites of robotic organizations and

competitions. *See the Appendix for suggested listings.*
- Go to robotics camp, or seek opportunities for summer employment or internships with engineering firms or government research laboratories.
- Visit the U.S. Department of Labor website for information on career opportunities, growth trends, and salary ranges.
- Talk to your school's principal about bringing robotics to your school, if it is not already a part of your school program.

You are writing the script for your future. You should make it as interesting and engaging as possible.

APPENDIX

Glossary of Robotic Terms

Actuator — A power mechanism used to create motion of the robot; a device that converts electrical, hydraulic, or pneumatic energy into robot motion.

Autonomous – not controlled by outside forces – self controlled by means of sensors and programmed instructions.

Controller — Any piece of control hardware that allows you to control the robot (joystick, emergency-stop button, a start button, or a selector switch.)

Emergency Stop — The operation of a circuit using hardware-based components that overrides all other robot controls, removes drive power from the robot actuators, and causes all moving parts to stop.

End-effector — A device or tool connected to the robot arm or wrist. (Examples may include gripper, spot-weld gun, arc-weld gun, spray-paint gun, or any other application tools.)

Energy Source - Any electrical, mechanical, hydraulic, pneumatic, chemical, thermal, or other source of power.

Gripper – a type of end effector

Hazardous Motion – Any motion that is likely to cause personal physical harm.

Industrial Robot – A reprogrammable, multifunctional manipulator designed to move material, parts, tools, or specialized devices through variable programmed motions for the performance of a variety of tasks.

Maintenance – The act of keeping the robots and robot systems in their proper operating condition.

Mobile Robot – A self-propelled and self-contained robot that is capable of moving. Can be a ground, aerial or marine robot.

Motor – a rotating machine that changes electrical energy to mechanical energy; the primary output device for the robot

Operator — The person controlling the robot.

Program

1. (noun) A sequence of instructions to be executed by the computer or robot controller to control a robot or robot system.

2. (verb) to furnish (a computer) with a code of instruction.

3. (verb) to teach a robot system a specific set of movements and instructions to accomplish a task.

Repair — To restore robots and robot systems to operating condition after damage, malfunction, or wear.

Remote control — enables you to control your robot from a distance by sending it direct commands.

Robot — A machine or device that operates automatically or any machine that can be programmed to carry out instructions and perform particular duties, especially one that can take over tasks normally done by people.

Robotic Engineer — A person who designs, maintains, and researches new applications for robots.

Robot Manufacturer — A company or business involved in either the design, fabrication, or sale of robots, robot tooling, robotic peripheral equipment or controls, and associated equipment.

Safeguard — A barrier guard, device, or safety procedure designed for the protection of people.

Safety Procedure — An instruction designed for the protection of people.

Sensor — A device that responds to physical stimuli (such as heat, light, sound, pressure, magnetism, motion, etc.) and transmits the resulting signal or data for providing a measurement, operating a control, or both.

Service — To adjust, repair, or maintain a robot.

Servo — an electromechanical device that allows robot parts to pivot

Service robot — machines that extend human capabilities.

Tetrix — Robotic prototyping kit made by Pitsco

Robotic Competitions

A few of the more popular competitions include

- Boosting Engineering, Science, and Technology (BEST). A robotic competition that provides students with an intense, hands-on, real engineering and problem-solving experience that is also fun. (www.bestinc.org)

- DARPA Grand Challenge (www.darpa.mil/grandchallenge)

- EARLY Robotics Competition - A robotics program for elementary school students. (www.earlyrobotics.org)

- FIRA RoboWorld Cup - FIRA is most for above BA/BS level students and companies to develop their research in robotic field though robot soccer. (www.fira.net)

- FIRST LEGO League (www.firstlegoleague.org)

- FIRST Robotics Competition. High-tech robot sporting event for high school students. (www.usfirst.org)

- GEAR Robotics Competition (www.gearrobotics.org)

- Intelligent Ground Vehicle Competition (IGVC) - The IGVC challenges student teams to develop an autonomous ground vehicle that can navigate a complex list of mobility, design, and interoperable architecture requirements. (www.auvsifoundation.org/igvc)

- International Aerial Robotics Competition (IARC) - The AUVSI International Aerial Robotics Competition, now in its 22nd year, involves the development of sophisticated aerial robots attempting a never-before-achieved mission to fly indoors to covertly search for and retrieve a specific target. Key to the Competition mission is that these flying robots are fully autonomous "thinking" machines. There will be no humans controlling the robots. They must avoid obstacles, navigate, and search for the target item without any human intervention or use of GPS navigation aides. (www.aerialroboticscompetition.org)

- International Autonomous Robot Contest (iaroc.org)

- International RoboBoat Competition - Student teams race autonomous surface vehicles (ASVs) of their own design through an aquatic obstacle course. (www.roboboat.org)

- International RoboSub Competition - RoboSub competition has advanced the development of autonomous underwater vehicles (AUVs) by challenging a new generation of engineers to perform realistic missions in a demanding underwater environment. The primary emphases of the competition are education and career preparation. Students gain an appreciation for the trade-offs inherent in any system design as well as lessons learned in transitioning from working bench prototype to operating reliably in the real world. (www. robosub.org)

- International Robot Olympiad - IROC is for students from under 8 to undergraduate students. (www.iroc.org)

- Marine Advanced Technology Education Center - Underwater Robotics Competition. (www.marinetech.org/rov-competition)

- National Robotics Challenge - The National Robotics Challenge contests are open to students in 6th grade through graduate school. (thenrc.org)

- National Underwater Robotics Challenge -The mission of the National Underwater Robotics Challenge is to bring science and technology educational opportunities to the students of all ages across the country. (www.h2orobots.org)

- Robo-Expo Competition - The Robo Expo is an event for students of all ages, with a shared interest in robotics, to come together to pursue similar goals or express themselves uniquely. Participation in Robo Expo is open to schools, home school groups, clubs, and any children sponsored by an adult. Robo Expo exhibits are open to all robotics kits—NXT, EV3, RCX, Arduino, Wedo, Hummingbirds, and anything else. (www.robo-expo.org)

- RoboCup Challenge - By the middle of the 21st century, a team of fully autonomous humanoid robot soccer players shall win a soccer game, complying with the official rules of FIFA, against the winner of the most recent World Cup. (www.robocup.org)

- Robocup Junior - Project-oriented educational robotics for students up through age 19, with a focus on providing a hands-on, scaffolded environment where learners can grow--by expanding their knowledge of, sparking their curiosity about and increasing their comfort with technology (rcj.robocup.org)

- Robofest - Robofest is a festival of competitions and events with autonomous robots that encourages students to have fun while learning principles of physical science, computer science, technology, engineering, and math (STEM), and Information and Communication Technologies (ICT). Students design, construct, and program the robots. Any robotics kits are allowed in the construction of robots. (www.robofest.net)

- RoboGames - The best minds from around the world compete in over 50 different events: combat robots, fire-fighters, LEGO bots, hockey bots, walking humanoids, soccer bots, sumo bots, and even androids that do kung-fu. Some robots are autonomous, some are remote controlled - but they're all cool! As an open event, anyone can compete (robogames.net)

- SeaPerch - Each year, middle and high school students from across the country gather to compete in the National SeaPerch Challenge. During the National SeaPerch Challenge, student teams must demonstrate the capabilities of the SeaPerches they have built as they navigate through an underwater obstacle course. Teams also display posters and deliver oral presentations about their design philosophy and construction challenges before a panel of judges. SeaPerch is an easy to assemble, underwater ROV (remotely operated vehicle) which is built from a kit. (seaperch.org).

- Student Unmanned Air Systems (SUAS) Competition - The SUAS Competition, aimed at stimulating and fostering interest in unmanned air systems, technologies and careers, focuses on the design, integration, and demonstration of a system capable of conducting air operations which includes autonomous flight, navigation of a specified course, and use of onboard payload sensors. (www.auvsifoundation.org/suas)

- The VEX IQ Challenge, presented by the Robotics Education & Competition Foundation, is a brand new STEM program for elementary and middle school students (ages 8-14, vex.com).

- The VEX Robotics Competition, presented by the Robotics Education & Competition Foundation, is the ultimate STEM activity for middle school and high school students (ages 11-18). (vex.com)

- The TSA-VEX Robotics Competition provides students with a hands-on, co-curricular competition for learning about science, technology, engineering and mathematics (STEM) and complements the existing technology-related competitions offered by TSA. (vex.com)

- VEX U takes the VEX Robotics Competition to the next level for university students (ages 18+). VEX U teams participate in VEX Skyrise, but with a few twists. The rules for the VEX U version of VEX Skyrise will be available in early June, so check back often. In addition to having a great time and building amazing robots, through their participation in VEX U students get to apply the theoretical STEM knowledge they learn in their college courses, while picking-up many of the academic and life skills necessary to excel in the work force. (vex.com)

- Trinity College Fire-Fighting Contest - One of the world's best known and long-lived international robot competitions, the low-cost annual Trinity College Fire Fighting Home Robot Contest (TCFFHRC) challenge is to build a fully autonomous robot that can navigate through a maze resembling the floor plan of a house, locate a burning candle and extinguish the flame in the shortest amount of time. (www.trincoll.edu/events/robot)

- Trinity College RoboWaiter Contest - The RoboWaiter contest challenges teams to design autonomous service robots to aid individuals with mobility impairment. RoboWaiter is unique because it relies on real people with disabilities in its planning and execution. (www.trincoll.edu/events/robot)

For a current and more comprehensive list of competitions, visit the Engineering Education Service Center's website: www.engineeringedu.com.

Recommended Reading

Accreditation Board for Engineering and Technology (ABET) website: www. abet.org

Baine, Celeste. "Is There an Engineer Inside You?: A Comprehensive Guide to Career Decisions in Engineering." Eugene, OR: Engineering Education Service Center, 2014.

— — —. "The Green Engineer: Engineering Careers to Save the Earth." Eugene, OR: Engineering Education Service Center, 2011.

— — —. "Ideas in Action: A Girl's Guide to Careers in Engineering." Eugene, OR: Engineering Education Service Center, 2009.

— — —. "The Musical Engineer: A Music Enthusiast's Guide to Careers in Music Engineering and Technology." Eugene, OR: Engineering Education Service Center, 2007.

— — —. "The Maritime Engineer: Careers in Naval Architecture and Marine, Ocean and Naval Engineering." Eugene, OR: Engineering Education Service Center, 2010.

— — —. "The Fantastical Engineer: A Thrillseeker's Guide to Careers in Theme Park Engineering." Second Ed. Eugene, OR: Engineering Education Service Center, 2007.

— — —. "High Tech Hot Shots: Careers in Sports Engineering." Alexandria, VA: National Society of Professional Engineers, 2004.

— — —. "Marine Engineering Teacher's Guide." Pittsburg, KS: Pitsco Education, 2012

— — —. "TETRIX® MAX Autonomous Robotics Engineering Teacher's Guide." Pittsburg, KS: Pitsco Education, 2010.

— — —. "TETRIX® MAX R/C Robotics Engineering Teacher's Guide." Pittsburg, KS: Pitsco Education, 2010

Bolles, Richard Nelson. "What Color is your Parachute?: A Practical Manual for Job Hunters and Career Changers." Berkeley: Ten Speed Press, 2001.

Bridgman, Roger. "Robot: Discover the Amazing World of Machines, from Robots that Play Chess to Systems the Think." New York, NY: DK Publishing, 2004.

Brockman, Reed. "From Sundaes to Space Stations: Careers in Civil Engineering." Eugene, OR: Bonamy Publishing, 2010.

Bruno Siciliano, Oussama Khatib, "Springer Handbook of Robotics," Springer-Verlag New York, Inc., Secaucus, NJ, 2007

Holmquist, Stephanie, "A multi-case study of student interactions with educational robots and impact on Science, Technology, Engineering, and Math (STEM) learning and attitudes" (2014). Graduate Theses and Dissertations. http://scholarcommons.usf.edu/etd/5043

iRobot website: www.irobot.com

Murphy, Robin. "Disaster Robotics." Cambridge, MA: The MIT Press, 2014.

National Aeronautics and Space Administration website: nasa.gov

Robotics Academy at the National Robotics Engineering Consortium website: www.rec.ri.cmu.edu/education

Society of Naval and Marine Engineers (SNAME) website: www.sname.org

Winfield, Alan. "Robotics: A Very Short Introduction." Oxford, United Kingdom: Oxford University Press, 2012.

Worcester Polytechnic University website: wpi.edu

Index

Engineering Careers App

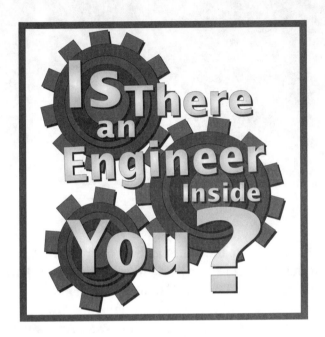

Includes:

- **40** Engineering and Technology Descriptions
- **40** Videos About the Types of Engineering
- **Salary** Information
- **Job** Outlook for Each Discipline
- **College** Directory
- **Scholarships**

Figure out what kind of engineer you want to be!

Only for iPhone. Available at iTunes

About the Author

Celeste Baine, is a biomedical engineer, Director of the Engineering Education Service Center and the award-winning author of over twenty books and booklets on engineering careers and education. She won the Norm Augustine Award from the National Academy of Engineering (The Norm Augustine award is given to an engineer who has demonstrated the capacity for communicating the excitement and wonder of engineering). She also won the American Society for Engineering Education's Engineering Dean Council's Award for the Promotion of Engineering Education and Careers, and is listed on the National Engineers Week website as one of 50 engineers you should meet. The National Academy of Engineering has included Celeste in their Gallery of Women Engineers and she has been named one of the Nifty-Fifty individuals who have made a major impact on the field of engineering by the USA Science and Engineering Festival. She has spent the past 15 years advising students and parents on the challenges and benefits of obtaining an engineering degree.